Making Great Memories

The Date Night Collection Vol 1

LC GREATOREX

Copyright © 2017 by Lisa C Greatorex

All rights reserved. No part of this book may be reproduced or transmitted in any form or by any means, electronic or mechanical, including photocopying, recording or by any information storage and retrieval system, without written permission from the author.

Disclaimer
The methods described within this book are the author's personal thoughts. They are not intended to be a definitive set of instructions. Neither the publisher, distributor nor the author shall be liable for any physical, psychological, emotional, financial, or commercial damages, including, but not limited to, special, incidental, consequential or other damages by the information contained in this book. The decision to use a product or follow a suggestion in this book is the sole responsibility of the reader. This book is presented solely for motivational, educational and entertainment purposes only.

Cover Design: Vila Design
Formatting: Polgarus Studio

*This book is dedicated to my husband, Jim,
the most loving and passionate man I have ever known.*

Contents

Introduction 1

How To Use This Book 3

Making Great Memories Pantry 7

Making Great Memories Kitchen 10

Chapter 1: Tropical Island Staycation 14

Chapter 2: Valentine's Day with a French Twist 28

Chapter 3: Spring Into Love With Golf 46

Chapter 4: Frugal Fun Friday 60

Chapter 5: When A Man Loves A Woman (Man Plan) 82

Chapter 6: From Palette To Palate 98

Chapter 7: Anniversary Quickie 116

Chapter 8: Japaneasy 126

Chapter 9: Role Play Getaway: Cowboy Up! 140

Chapter 10: Role Play Getaway: Italian Style 154

Chapter 11: Play Together, Stay Together 162

Chapter 12: British Birthday Invasion 174

Recipe Index 184

Final Thoughts 189

About The Author 191

Acknowledgments and Gratitude 193

Introduction

Do you remember when you first met your partner and it felt like a million butterflies were fluttering in your stomach? Do you long to feel that same feeling again? Would you believe me if I told you it's still possible to create a lifetime of butterflies?

Before I explain, let's be realistic for a moment. Life happens. We spend our early adult years in and out of relationships until, eventually, we find the *one*. Then we have children, financial responsibilities, careers, and a home to manage, all of which, while exciting, can take a heavy toll on our marriages. Busyness becomes the enemy of our relationships. Eventually, we learn that it isn't what we do that matters most, but how much we give of ourselves to our partner. With the current divorce rate at fifty percent, I think there's an urgent need for learning how to keep the lines of communication open in our relationships, and for finding creative ways to keep the spark alive forever.

This is a book you NEED to have in your relationship toolbox. In *Making Great Memories*, you will learn how to:

- **Be a creative and fun partner.** Not only with your lover—your creativity and enthusiasm for life will spill over into relationships with family and friends.

- **Keep the spark.** You will learn what intimacy feels like and how always to maintain desire.

- **Stay committed to sex.** Learn how premeditated, willful and intentional lovemaking leads to a lifetime of fidelity.

- **Make Great Memories.** This book will teach you how to create special memories with the people you love—memories you'll cherish for a lifetime.

Making Great Memories is a detailed guide to creating intimate memories through themed date nights. Although the themes in this volume are intended to be experienced with a significant other, they can also be adapted to create memories with friends and family. Each date night starts with creating the right atmosphere, and includes tips on how to dress, what music to play, ideas for couple fun-time in and out of the bedroom, snuggle-time suggestions and gift ideas, and, of course, meal recommendations! Each theme includes recipes for a happy hour cocktail and appetizer, as well as a main course and dessert. These themes have been broken up into ideas for holidays and seasons, birthdays, role-play-getaways, and just-for-fun quickies.

Please don't be overwhelmed with the amount of material provided or think you have to incorporate every suggestion in order to create a successful experience. I always say: "Take what you want and leave the rest." You certainly don't need to use every suggestion at once. Save it for another time, because there WILL be another time. I guarantee that you'll have just as much fun planning the theme as you'll have with the experience. When your loved one looks at you with tears in his or her eyes and says, "No one has ever done anything like this for me in my entire life," that's when you realize how fulfilling a relationship can be! Taking the time to create an experience for another human being is a true measure of love.

I believe the most important lesson we can learn while we're here on this Earth is how to love, and we can only learn how to love through relationships. The greatest gift you can give someone is your time, so I invite you to start planning your first theme. Get ready to experience the magical flutter of butterflies once again! After trying a couple of themes from this book, you may even find your inner "theme queen" and be inspired to create your own theme idea. If you do, please share it with us at www.makinggreatmemories.com.

Love,

LC

How To Use This Book

The Most Important Goal

The primary purpose of this book is just to have FUN! To achieve this, you may need to step out of your comfort zone and allow yourself to be a little vulnerable. When you and your partner open up to one another with these unique themes, magic happens, and intimacy grows in your relationship. It doesn't matter if you are laying the foundation early in a new relationship or reviving one that's become stagnant over the years; we are all looking for new ways to have fun with our partners. One of the biggest lessons I've learned in life is not to take myself so seriously. Learning to let go of expectations and being flexible, will open the pathway for more FUN in all your relationships. As you will learn from my experiences, anything can happen and perfection rarely exists. Allow the playful you to emerge and know that the fun happens when you just "roll with it" and enjoy living in the moment.

Theme Nights

Although these ideas come in the form of date nights, they can be used anytime and for any occasion (not just with a partner). Consider adapting themes for fun with friends and family. It's become my personal pattern to do a themed date night once a month, usually on a Friday night, but I often do a "quickie" date night whenever I feel the need to "spice" things up, or just to turn an ordinary day into an extraordinary one. *Making Great Memories* isn't a book about party planning or recognizing significant life events; this is a book celebrating intimate relationships and creating lasting memories amid the daily grind of life.

Host a "Queen of Theme" Party for Girlfriends

Hosting a "Queen of Theme" party for girlfriends is a fantastic way to introduce the concept of *Making Great Memories*. Planning and sharing is an opportunity to strengthen our sisterhood and bond together over conversation and laughter. This book will become a catalyst for your creativity. Gather with girlfriends and plan a theme date night calendar, share your tools and materials, arrange childcare for one another; great friends are essential to making great memories happen. My blog at www.makinggreatmemories.com/blog/ has a theme party planned just for you! Finally, a "book club" that you and your girlfriends can truly relax and enjoy.

Food and Recipes

Food makes the memory, but that stress shouldn't cause us to avoid date nights. There are three ways to approach date night meals. **1. The Easy Way.** Take advantage of your local grocery store, which often offers a variety of delicious choices: buffets and salad bars, pre-made items like sushi, seasoned meats and fish, precut vegetables, a full-service bakery, and a deli that will often customize orders if you ask. Grocery stores have evolved over the years, so take advantage of the convenience. **2. The LC Way.** I love to cook (and I especially love to eat) but I don't want to spend all my time in the kitchen. The recipes I chose for this book are quick and easy to prepare, cost-efficient, match the theme, and taste great! **3. The "Take It Up A Notch" Way.** For readers who want to challenge themselves in the kitchen, many themes suggest a few celebrity chefs whose recipes fit nicely with the genre.

Making Great Memories Toolbox

To assist in your planning and preparation for each theme, I have included a Making Great Memories Toolbox at the end of every chapter. To give you an idea, see my toolbox of the most commonly used items for *Making Great Memories* at the conclusion of this section. For those who love to learn through photo and video tutorials, you'll find links to helpful resources, including my website www.makinggreatmemories.com, and social media, interspersed throughout this book.

Finally, I have included a blank page at the end of every chapter where you can take notes and record your great memories.

So are you ready to have some fun? Let's get started!

Making Great Memories Toolbox

(Commonly used items)

Many of the following items can be found at:

www.makinggreatmemories.com/shop/

LED tealights - several to use for home and travel
Red light bulbs
Portable music and speaker system
8-10 yards of inexpensive sheer fabric (for temporary bed canopy)
Coffee table
Large serving tray
Table settings for two (including pretty glasses, dishes, linens, etc.)
Martini shaker and glasses
Appetizer plates with fun cocktail napkins
Themed lingerie
An open mind and a good imagination!

Making Great Memories Pantry

At first, setting up a well-stocked pantry may seem expensive and a bit overwhelming, but it's truly a worthwhile investment. Many of these items will be in your pantry for years. You'll always be prepared, you'll be more likely to cook and, most importantly, you'll be ready to make great memories!

Baking Cupboard
    All-purpose flour
    Granulated sugar
    Confectioner's sugar
    Brown sugar
    Baking soda
    Baking powder
    Fine salt
    Honey
    Pure vanilla extract
    Shortening
    Vinegars: apple cider, balsamic, red wine, rice vinegar or mirin
    Sesame oil
    Soy sauce, Tabasco, Sriracha, Worcestershire
    Unsweetened cocoa powder, baking chocolate
    Chocolate morsels
    Coconut flakes
    Variety of dried herbs and spices
    Nonstick cooking spray

Refrigerator
- Dairy: milk, light cream, heavy cream, sour cream, yogurt, whipped cream, unsalted butter
- Variety cheeses: feta, cheddar, blue, gorgonzola, goat, cream cheese, mozzarella, parmesan
- Eggs
- Mayonnaise
- Mustard: dijon, whole grain, yellow
- Ketchup
- Produce: avocado, carrots, colored peppers, onions, green onion, shallots, garlic, celery, cauliflower, broccoli, leafy greens(kale, spinach) mushrooms, variety of lettuces, beets, squash
- Variety of potatoes tiny, red, gold, russet, fingerling
- Variety of tomatoes cherry, roma, beefsteak
- Lemons
- Limes
- Apples
- Ginger root
- Champagne

Pantry Cupboard
- Long grain white rice and brown rice
- Variety of dry pasta
- Dry breadcrumbs, panko crumbs
- Variety crackers
- Old fashioned rolled oats
- Variety olives
- Jars of pickled jalapeno, red peppers, artichokes
- Salsa
- Variety canned tomatoes and paste
- Canned chickpeas, beans
- Nuts: almonds, walnuts, pecans, pine nuts

Freezer
- Shrimp
- Salmon
- Chicken, boneless breasts
- Ground beef and turkey
- Bacon, pancetta, proscuitto
- Bread
- Variety vegetables
- Variety fruit and berries
- Vanilla ice cream
- Coffee

Near the stove
- Extra virgin olive oil
- Vegetable oil
- Kosher salt and fresh ground pepper

On the window sill or grown near the kitchen door
- Fresh parsley, basil, thyme, mint, cilantro, rosemary, oregano, chives

Liquor Cabinet
- Gin
- White and dark rum
- Vodka
- Bourbon
- Tequila
- Red and white wine

Making Great Memories Kitchen

You are more likely to cook and make great memories if your kitchen is well-organized and clean. A kitchen is most functional if it's set up into 5 zones, but because all kitchens are different, it's really about what makes you most comfortable. Here is a suggestion for a well-organized kitchen and some tools to assist you in success.

Tips for Safety and Cleanliness

- Keep knives sharp
- Keep pot holders and oven mitts near the stove with a fire extinguisher close by
- Frequently wash your surfaces (cutting boards, counter, stove, oven in and out, inside refrigerator)
- Frequently wash your hands during meal preparation
- Rinse all fruits and vegetables, as well as chicken and fish
- Keep hot foods hot and cold foods cold
- Follow expiration dates
- Stay focused. Don't get distracted with phone calls or alcohol during food preparation and use a timer!

Kitchen Zones

Zone 1 Prepping- This area is for chopping, mixing etc. Have a safe place for your recipes, cookbook or ebook. Knives and cutting boards, all mixing and measuring equipment, basic ingredients for baking (like flour, sugar, spices etc.) in drawers or cupboards near this area.

Zone 2 Cooking- This is your stove area. Keep it clear and safe. Pot holders and cooling racks near by. Because they are used frequently during cooking, keep oils, salt and pepper near the cooking station. Keep a crock of frequently used cooking utensils near the stove area. This would include, flippers, wooden spoons, tongs etc. Baking pans, cookie sheets, pots and pans stored nearby.

Zone 3 Clean Up- This is the sink area. It helps to have a dishwasher. Otherwise, frequently-used items like pots, pans and knives still need to be washed daily. Use HOT water to wash and rinse. Wash dishes preferably with a clean dishcloth and not sponges (which can harbor bacteria). Have soap for hand washing and use separate towels for drying hands and dishes. Throw out garbage daily, compost and please recycle.

Zone 4 Food Serving- Keep all dinner dishes, bowls, serving platters, drinking glasses, silverware and napkins in the same general area of your kitchen, preferably close to the dining table.

Zone 5 Storage- It's great if you have the luxury of a pantry or lots of cupboard space. If space is limited, research kitchen organizers and other ways to maximize your space. This zone is where we store pantry foods and other items like plastic wrap, storage containers and kitchen towels.

Basic Kitchen Tools

- The best quality cooking pots and pans you can afford, cast iron skillet, nonstick skillet
- The best knives you can afford, especially a chef knife and paring knife
- Roasting pan, cookie sheet, 8x8 and 9x13 baking pans, loaf pan, cake pans, pie plate
- Various sizes of mixing bowls and prep bowls
- Measuring spoons, dry measuring cups, liquid measuring cup

Cutting boards
Cooling racks
Colander
Whisk, tongs, narrow metal spatula, flipper, rubber scraper, ladle, slotted spoon, wooden spoon, cheese grater, zester, mandoline, vegetable peeler
Mallet or meat tenderizer
Kitchen shears
Rolling pin
Can opener
Wine opener

1

Tropical Island Staycation

Aloha!

Winter feels very long in many parts of the country. Shorter days mean less sunshine and, consequently, less vitamin D. This lack of light and vitamins, compounded by our tendency to hibernate from the world when it's cold, can lead to a host of problems, including lack of exercise, weight gain, or seasonal depression. We need a vacation! Since jetting-off to a tropical island isn't a practical or affordable option for most, bringing home a little slice of paradise for an evening may be just the solution!

This theme is an excellent way to relive a honeymoon, since many couples celebrate their new marriage by honeymooning in a tropical destination. If that was the case for you, imagine how memorable it could be to get out the honeymoon album or make a photo slideshow to watch together. This theme could also be an excellent opportunity to surprise your loved one with plans for a future trip to return to paradise and renew your marriage vows.

I save this theme night for when I know I'll be stuck home for an entire day in a snowstorm. I listen to island music all day and cook throughout the evening. I build a massive fire in my woodstove and get the house really warm, then I dig deep into my summer clothing and pull out something I haven't worn since Labor Day. Lastly, I slather on a little suntan oil and the smell instantly transports me to a tropical paradise.

Creating your Tropical Paradise:

As in many of the upcoming themes, we're going to create three spaces for our tropical experience. First, the living room for cocktails, then the dining area for dinner in paradise, and, most importantly, the tropical fantasy suite.

The fantasy suite begins with mosquito netting hung above the bed. If that's not possible, use sheer fabric draped over the headboard and down the sides of the bed. If you have a canopy bed, consider sheer curtains around the frame, with a light fan blowing the curtains, just as you would experience in the tropics. White sheets (bamboo sheets) and a matching bedspread tie the tropical look together. Place silk (or real) tropical flowers around the room. I often add artificial blooms in the pot with my real plants. Many home and garden centers carry orchids year round if you want an exotic look. A large tropical houseplant would be great if you want to add more ambiance. Add LED or real candles in exotic aromas or try a plug-in air freshener in coconut or another tropical fragrances. For my last tropical island staycation, I used air fresheners in all three rooms to truly transport me southwards. Refer to the Tropical Island Staycation video at http://www.makinggreatmemories.com/videos to see how this look can be achieved.

For music, choose soothing background ocean waves, or island calypso, or both! Make a colorful sign to hang on the door that reads, "Fantasy Suite," or if you have a banner from the resort you stayed at on your honeymoon, hang that across the doorway.

It's 5 O'Clock Somewhere!

A cocktail hour could take place in your living room or even in the Fantasy Suite. Consider being goofy and sitting in beach chairs or on beach blankets. Wear your bikini and speedo! Set your chairs facing the television and watch your vacation pictures or one of the tropical movie suggestions. You can also set up an exotic coffee table with colorful flowers and a floating candle in a shallow bowl with sand and seashells. Add a bucket of a tropical beer like La Cerveza La Tropical, SanTan Pineapple or Corona. Set out any pictures you may have from a previous tropical vacation, or perhaps guidebooks to explore a future destination. Dream of all the tropical places you'd like to visit, and one in particular that you might get to explore together in the future. Drink your cocktails out of a souvenir glass or coconut and garnish it with fresh fruit and a paper umbrella.

The Romantic Dinner:

The dinner table should reflect the tropical theme as well. Find inexpensive floral napkins and bamboo placemats, or colorful plates from a secondhand store—keep in mind, nothing has to match! Use souvenir glasses from a previous trip or wooden tiki cups. Add flowers, candles, and tropical fruits to pull the look together. If you can, find a bottle of crisp white wine with a tropical label.

The Tropical Beat:

Consider calypso music, reggae, The Beach Boys, and Jimmy Buffet, or even the Elvis soundtrack from *Paradise, Hawaiian Style*. Amazon and iTunes have great tropical dance music to purchase. You can also stream music live from radio stations in Hawaii and the Caribbean. Have your music playing from room to room as you move through your night and possibly change the genre between each one.

Resort Wear:

You probably already have a tropical sundress you could wear for cocktails and dinner. Ask your partner to put on a tropical island shirt as well and maybe a Panama hat. Bathing suits are always acceptable and encouraged. Put a flower in your beach-curled hair, get a spray tan and wear the pleasant scent of suntan lotion. Paint your toenails a bright tropical color and go barefoot. Don't forget sunglasses. If looking for additional "fantasy suite" clothing and accessories, go to www.makinggreatmemories.com/shop/ for links to my tropical favorites.

Couple Fun Time:

You're now ready for fun, but you still have to set the tone. As soon as he walks through the door, place a lei around his neck and plant your sun-kissed lips on his. Research his name in Hawaiian and give him a new name for the evening, as well as your own! (For example James =Kimo and Lisa= Lika). Have his resort clothes ready or let him know what he needs to do to prepare for the special evening. Greet him with an island cocktail or dance together to your favorite tropical music. Challenge yourself to learn how to Hula

MAKING GREAT MEMORIES

Dance and show off your sensuality and grace. (There are many how-to videos on YouTube). You've already forgotten about the snow outside, and now it's time for your honey to forget it too!

Dinner in Paradise:

This is a "semi-homemade" dinner menu that is simple and delicious. If you want to "turn up the heat" in your kitchen, I suggest visiting Tropicalchefs.com where you will find fabulous tropical recipes and pictures.

The Tropical Dinner Menu

Cocktail
Piña Colada (leave out rum for a Virgin Colada)

Appetizer:
Coconut Shrimp with Easy Tropical Salsa

Dinner:
Island Teriyaki Chicken
Caribbean Rice
Grilled Mixed Vegetables

Dessert:
Warm Banana in Rum Sauce with Coconut Ice Cream
and Macadamia Nut Sprinkle

Recipes

Piña Colada

Nothing tastes more tropical than the creamy deliciousness of the Piña Colada! Serve it in a souvenir glass from a tropical vacation. Leave out the rum for a nonalcoholic version. Other tropical cocktail suggestions: Blue Hawaii, Mojito, Mai Tai and Cayman Lemonade.

Serves 2

Ingredients:
- 1 ½ cup ice
- ½ cup frozen pineapple
- ¼ cup pineapple juice
- ¼ cup coconut cream
- 2 oz white rum
- 1 oz dark rum

Directions:

1. Place all ingredients into a blender and blend until smooth. Pour into two souvenir glasses or sling glasses and garnish with pineapple slice, maraschino cherry and whipped cream.

Coconut Shrimp with Tropical Salsa

Coconut shrimp is the perfect starter for your tropical happy hour, and it's quite easy to prepare. I provided a recipe for the Caribbean Jerk seasoning, but when traveling, consider purchasing an inexpensive souvenir of a local flavor (often purchased just before departure at the airport). It's fun to remember vacations with flavorings like vanilla from Mexico, hot sauce from the Southwest or Caribbean Jerk seasoning from the Bahamas.

Serves 2

Ingredients:

½ pound large raw shrimp, peeled and deveined, keep tails
2 egg whites
2 T cornstarch
½ T Caribbean jerk seasoning* (recipe to follow)
1 cup flaked sweetened coconut
½ cup Japanese breadcrumbs (panko)
½ tsp paprika

Directions:

1. Preheat oven 425 degrees F. Lightly coat a wire rack on a baking pan with nonstick cooking spray.
2. Rinse and dry the shrimp. Leave tails on and devein.
3. In a shallow bowl, mix the egg whites until foamy using a whisk.
4. Place the cornstarch and jerk seasoning in another shallow dish.
5. Stir together the coconut, panko crumbs and paprika in a third shallow dish.
6. Dredge each shrimp one at a time in the cornstarch mixture, then the egg whites followed by the coconut. Place on greased wire rack and lightly coat the shrimp with the cooking spray.

7. Bake at 425 degrees F for 10-12 minutes until the shrimp is bright pink and the coconut is toasted. Flip the shrimp halfway through cooking time. Serve with dipping sauce (recipe below).

*Caribbean Jerk Seasoning

1 T allspice
¼ tsp cinnamon
¼ tsp cloves
¼ tsp cumin
1 tsp red pepper flakes
¼ cup brown sugar
¼ tsp salt and ⅛ tsp pepper
2 T canola oil

Directions:
Mix all ingredients in a small bowl and store in a plastic container.

Coconut Shrimp Dipping Sauces:

Easy Tropical Salsa - Take your favorite salsa and mix with grilled pineapple and mango. Sprinkle with chopped red onion.
Orange Dipping Sauce - In a small dish, mix orange marmalade with dijon mustard, honey and a little kick of hot sauce warmed in the microwave.

Island Teriyaki Chicken for Two

This is my "go to" dinner all year round. It is so easy to prepare with a nice presentation and pleases everyone at your dinner table. It's also an excellent choice for large gatherings.

Ingredients:
- 2 boneless chicken breasts
- Favorite store purchased Island Teriyaki Marinade
- Pineapple slices from the can (save juice for rice)

Directions:

1. Wash the chicken and dry with paper towels.
2. Pound the chicken breasts evenly and fairly thin. Place in a plastic reclosable storage bag. Add the marinade (enough to cover the chicken) and refrigerate until ready to cook. The longer, the more favor.
3. Heat grill or stovetop grill pan to med-high, grill chicken until cooked through - 160 degrees with a meat thermometer. Also, grill the pineapple slices directly on the grill. Serve alongside rice and vegetables.

Caribbean Rice with Mixed Vegetables

While the chicken is cooking, prepare the rice according to directions. If not using a purchased box of Caribbean rice, create your own using rice mixed with water, pineapple juice and jerk seasoning. When the rice is done cooking, add pineapple tidbits and a tablespoon of flaked coconut. For a pretty presentation, pack the rice into a large biscuit cutter or ramekin sprayed lightly with nonstick spray so it comes out in a cute design on the plate.

Serves 2

Ingredients:
½ red pepper chopped
1 small red onion sliced or chopped
1 zucchini chopped
4 oz whole button mushrooms cleaned and cut in half
1 T olive oil
1 tsp Kosher salt and few turns of freshly ground pepper

Directions:
1. Preheat oven to 425 degrees F or grill on med-high.
2. Place all vegetables in a bowl and mix with olive oil, salt and pepper.
3. Place on a baking sheet or grill pan and roast vegetables about 15 minutes; don't overcook.

Assemble the grilled chicken with a slice or two of grilled pineapple, serve alongside a tower of Caribbean rice and roasted vegetables.

Warm Banana in Rum Sauce with Coconut Ice cream and Macadamia Sprinkle

This is a delicious dessert that can be made in a matter of minutes. It's wonderful to serve all year round, but I especially love it during a snowstorm. It can also be made by omitting the rum and increasing the water to ⅓ cup and adding a ½ tsp vanilla.

Serves 2

Ingredients:
- 2 T unsalted butter
- 2 very firm bananas sliced down the middle and then in half (total of 8 pieces)
- 2 T packed brown sugar
- 2 T dark or light rum
- ¼ cup water
- 1/8 tsp nutmeg
- ⅛ tsp cinnamon
- ⅛ tsp kosher salt
- 2 T chopped Macadamia nuts (pecans, pistachios or almonds are fine too)
- coconut ice cream

Directions:

1. Melt butter in heavy 10 inch skillet on medium-high. Remove from heat and add the brown sugar and rum, put back on burner and continue to stir until the sugar has melted.
2. Next, add the water, nutmeg, cinnamon and salt. Cook until sauce has thickened about 1- 2 minutes. Add the banana slices and coat with the sauce.
3. Serve bananas hot over coconut ice cream and sprinkle with Macadamia nuts.

Cuddle Time:

End your evening in paradise with one of these island-themed movies:

Pirates of the Caribbean
Cast Away
Dr. No
50 First Dates
Blue Lagoon
Paradise, Hawaiian Style
The Beach
Lilo & Stitch

Tropical Staycation Toolbox

Many of the following items can be found at:
www.makinggreatmemories.com/shop/

mosquito netting or sheer fabric
white sheets
tropical flowers or houseplants
exotic aromas from candles and air fresheners
tropical music
beach chairs, blankets, sand and shells
souvenir glasses
tropical (or colorful) dishes and table linens
resort wear, sundress, tropical shirt, bathing suit, sunglasses etc.
suntan lotion
Lei

Tropical Island Staycation video at
http://www.makinggreatmemories.com/videos

Notes & Memories

2

Valentine's Day with a French Twist

Introduction:

As February 14th approaches, a man often gets anxious over what to do for the woman in his life. Although many men think women desire love in the form of diamonds, chocolate, and roses—what most women truly desire is our man's focused attention. Go beyond the usual trinity of love and consider sharing an evening filled with intimacy and connection. The greatest gift you can give one another is your time.

I often associate Valentine's Day with the French, so it seemed fitting to create a theme dedicated to Paris, the city of love. Of course, you don't need to reserve this night just for Valentine's Day. If you are spending an evening at home and want to do something extra special, I think you will love these ideas for adding French flavor. I've even included a few main courses to choose from, so go ahead and repeat this theme a few times! Who would object to spending an evening dining on French cuisine or French kissing in a French Boudoir?

Bon Jour

When my partner and I discussed what we wanted to do for Valentine's Day, I told him I wanted to create a special evening at home just for the two of us. On the morning of Valentine's Day, I let my partner know the theme for our Valentine's night. First, I set out a placemat with croissants and fruit along with coffee made in my French press. I made a sweet Valentine's card with a Parisian theme and the words *Je t'aime* (I love you). Then I sent him off to work with a French kiss.

Atmosphere d'amour

As with many of my themes, I wanted to start in one place and finish in another. When I created this Valentine's evening, we were wintering for a month in the panhandle of Florida where the sunsets were magnificent. Even though it was very chilly on the night of Valentine's Day, I made hors d'oeuvres to take to the beach with my bébé. I created a beautiful picnic basket with a French cheese charcuterie board consisting of a baguette, soft Brie cheese, apples, grapes, fig jam and, of course, French wine. As a gift to your honey for Valentine's Day, consider a Laguiole folding knife. Begun in 1829, Laguiole knives are still handmade from start to finish in the Aubrac region of France by a single artisan. This item makes a lovely addition to any picnic basket. If you live in a warm climate, bring your picnic to a park. In colder climates, have your hors d'oeuvre picnic in front of a fire.

For our dinner atmosphere, I wanted to create a quaint bistro setting. Fortunately, the place we rented had a bistro table and chair set. If you don't have one, use the corner of your dining room table. Because it was Valentine's Day, I decorated the table in pinks, reds, and whites, but the Parisian way is to keep lines clean. A linen tablecloth with white plates would be striking. You can purchase Eiffel Tower wine glasses and champagne flutes online. Consider choosing French lavender as your flower arrangement or, in my case, roses given to me by my lover. Gentlemen, order flowers and have them delivered for an extra-special gesture. That way, she can have them displayed before you arrive. Be sure to include a bottle of Perrier or Evian water. Have your beautiful table set before the evening festivities begin. I had my partner sit at the table with a French 75 Martini while I put together our dinner.

La Musique

Because it's Valentine's, you have an abundance of music to choose from—tune in to your favorite online radio for ideas. I found French Cooking music, which was perfect. I also like Paris Combo radio, the Williams and Sonoma Paris CD, soundtracks from *Chocolat* and *Amélie* and, of course, there's always Cole Porter.

Haute Couture

The classic Parisian look is to wear a little black dress with ballet flats and an accent scarf. Think Audrey Hepburn returning from Paris in the classic movie

Sabrina. You can watch "how to" videos online to create the perfect French twist or, if you have short hair, find a cute barrette. There are also tutorials online for Audrey Hepburn makeup. I love her wing-tip eyes and straight-across eyebrows. A vital accessory for this night is your perfume! In France, all women wear perfume. They say the scent you dab defines who you are. So tonight, are you classic and refined or seductive and dangerous? To quote Coco Chanel, "A woman who doesn't wear perfume has no future." A classic French perfume like Chanel No. 5, Opium, Shalimar or Anais Anais is a perfect Valentine's Day gift from the gentleman to his valentine. Wear the scent behind your ears, on your wrists and even your clothes. French men also dress well and are fashion-conscious so, gentlemen, no casual wear tonight.

Rendezvous Romantique

After dinner, you may want to spend time like they do in France at the outdoor café writing each other poetry . . . or you could create a French Boudoir! Think Moulin Rouge or, in simpler American terms, the Red Room from *50 Shades of Grey*! A French Boudoir is a luxurious and seductive place that can be created using red satin sheets, lots of pillows, a hanging bed net, red light bulbs, lots of candles (I love the LED lights), peacock feathers, adult toys, etc. Watch my video at http://www.makinggreatmemories.com/videos to see how I created a French boudoir. Continue with the French music. You will also need to transform yourself from the clean, classy Parisian to a Femme Fatale (a dangerously attractive woman). If you are interested in dressing as a Parisian Showgirl from Moulin Rouge, a sexy French maid, or even wearing an Eiffel Tower dress, refer to my website at www.makinggreatmemories.com/shop/

Menu Français

French cuisine is delicious and elegant, but it doesn't have to be difficult. There are so many excellent culinary options, but I've selected meals that are simple and easy to prepare in advance. The evening is about you and your partner, so we don't want to spend too much time in the kitchen. If inspired

MAKING GREAT MEMORIES

to master more French cooking skills, consider using recipes from the famous television chefs Julia Child and Jacques Pepin.

Valentine's Day with a French Twist Menu

apéritif (The before dinner cocktail)
The French 75

Hors d'oeuvres (The appetizer at the beginning of a meal)
Baguette, French cheese like Brie, apples, grapes and fig jam

Soup Du Jour (Soup of the day)
French Onion Soup

Crudités (Assorted raw vegetables, typically with a vinaigrette)
Mixture of colorful vegetables served with a traditional French vinaigrette

Entree' (The main course of a meal)
Filet of Beef au Poivre
or
Chicken Cordon Bleu
All served with fingerling potatoes and haricots verts (French green beans)

Le désert (An end of the meal sweet)
Profiteroles

Digestif (After dinner drink that supposedly settles your stomach after a night of fine dining)
Cognacs and Brandy such as Calvados and Armagnac
Cafe' (Coffee)
Espresso
Cappuccino

Recipes

The French 75 Cocktail

Rumor has it that this cocktail was named in honor of the famous French 75 light field gun of World War I and was popularized by Harry's New York Bar in Paris. I like to present this special cocktail on a pretty tray with the gin syrup in a little pitcher and the champagne in an ice bucket.

Ingredients:
- 1/4 cup sugar
- 1/4 cup water
- 1/4 cup gin, preferably English dry gin
- 2 T fresh lemon juice
- 1 bottle champagne (chilled)
- garnish with lemon twist

Directions:

1. To make simple syrup, heat sugar and water in a small saucepan over medium heat, stirring until the sugar is dissolved. Cool.
2. Combine syrup with gin and lemon juice. Refrigerate.
3. In a chilled champagne flute, put 2 T gin simple syrup and slowly top off with champagne. Garnish with a lemon twist.

Simple French Onion Soup

This recipe is so easy and delicious. I often double the amount and freeze it to enjoy all winter long.

Serves: 4

Ingredients:
- 1 pound onions, sliced
- ¼ cup unsalted butter
- 2 sprigs fresh thyme
- Kosher salt and fresh ground pepper to taste
- 1 T flour
- ½ cup white wine
- 3 cups beef broth
- ½ pound Gruyere or Swiss cheese
- Baguette sliced and toasted

Directions:

1. Peel the onions and slice into thin half rounds.
2. In a heavy sauce pan, melt the butter on medium heat and then add the onions. Turn heat down to medium low and cook until onions are caramelized, about 30 minutes. Stir frequently.
3. Once the onions are golden, add the thyme, stripping the leaves from the twig, and add the salt and pepper.
4. Add the flour, turn heat up to medium and stir constantly.
5. Add the wine and broth, then bring to a simmer. Let it simmer for at least 30 minutes. The longer it sits the better it tastes.

Assemble:
Slice the baguette and toast. Ladle soup into crocks (I used heart-shaped crocks for Valentine's Day), topped with the baguette slices and then place a

few slices of Swiss cheese or Gruyere. Place crocks on a baking sheet and put under a broiler until cheese is bubbly and starts to brown. Carefully remove from broiling and serve on a napkin-lined plate with a sprig of thyme.

Crudité with Vinaigrette for Two

Take a platter and place small mounds of ingredients artfully around the plate. Ideally, it should be colorful and full of variety. Set out two small plates and proceed to put together your own salads and serve with the vinaigrette.

Suggestions for the crudité:
Chopped salad greens, grated carrots, sliced beets, sliced peppers (all colors) radish, celery, tomatoes, fennel, mushrooms, asparagus, herbs, fruit, hard-boiled egg slices, lentils. Anything!

Traditional Vinaigrette

Ingredients:
- 1 tsp Dijon mustard
- 1 tsp red wine vinegar
- 1 pinch kosher salt
- 3 T light vegetable oil
- pepper freshly ground
- 1 clove garlic peeled and cut in half

Directions:
In a small bowl, mix the first three ingredients and then slowly add the oil, stirring constantly until it emulsifies. Add the pepper and the garlic. Remove the garlic before serving.

Filet of Beef Au Poivre

Simple, yet impressive

Serves 2

Ingredients:
- 2 filet mignon a little over 1 inch thick
- kosher salt
- Fresh ground black pepper
- 2 T unsalted butter, divided
- 1 T olive oil
- 2 large shallots chopped (½ Cup)
- ½ cup beef broth
- ¼ cup cognac or brandy (this equals a nip, which is cheaper to purchase)

Directions:

1. Dry the filets with a paper towel and then sprinkle with salt and pepper on both sides. Let them sit to warm up a little.
2. In a sauté pan, heat 1T butter and 1T oil over medium high until the butter is melted.
3. Add the steaks and lower heat to medium.
4. Cook 4 minutes on one side, flip, and cook 3 min on the other side (for med rare).
5. Remove steaks and keep warm under aluminum foil.
6. Back in your sauté pan, add the shallots and cook 2 min on medium heat.
7. Add the beef broth and cook on high for 5 minutes. You want to reduce the liquid by half.
8. Add the cognac or brandy and cook 2 minutes more.
9. Finish with 1T butter and salt to taste.
10. Pour the sauce over the warm steak.

Chicken Cordon Bleu For Two

This recipe is baked for an easier and healthier version. It can also be prepared and refrigerated ahead of time, until ready to cook.

Ingredients:
- 2 boneless chicken breasts (rinse with water and pat dry with paper towel)
- kosher salt and fresh ground pepper
- 2 slices prosciutto or thin ham
- 2 slices gruyere or swiss cheese
- 1 egg beaten
- ½ cup dry bread crumbs
- 2 T butter (melted)
- 1 large shallot, minced
- ½ cup whipping cream
- 2 T butter

Directions:

1. With a cooking mallet, pound the chicken between two pieces of plastic wrap to ¼ inch.
2. Sprinkle with salt and pepper, then layer with ham and cheese.
3. Roll up tightly, then hold in place with toothpicks, a skewer or tie with kitchen twine.
4. Roll in beaten egg, then crumbs.
5. Place in a greased baking pan or individual casserole dish with seam side down.
6. Drizzle with melted butter and bake 350 degrees for 35 minutes.
7. While the chicken is baking, make the sauce.
8. Cordon Bleu Sauce: Chop 2 T shallots and sauté in 2 T butter for 10 minutes. Add ½ C whipping cream and keep warm on low until serving.
9. Before serving, remove the string, skewer or toothpicks from the chicken and cover with sauce.

Accompaniments

Fingerling Potatoes and Haricots Verts (French Green Beans)

Fingerling potatoes are interesting to look at on a plate, but you can also use any potato cut into bite-sized pieces. Haricots Verts aren't always available in a grocery store, but you can find tender whole green beans in most frozen food sections.

Fingerling Potatoes

Ingredients:

    ½ pound fingerlings, washed and sliced in half
    1 T olive oil
    kosher salt and fresh ground pepper

Directions:

1. Preheat oven 425 degrees F.
2. Place potatoes on a baking pan. Drizzle with the olive oil and salt and pepper. Toss with hands.
3. Turn all potatoes onto their cut side and bake for 30 minutes or until crisp and tender. Turn over potatoes halfway through cooking time.

Haricots Verts

Ingredients:

½ pound Haricots Verts or tender, thin green beans (trim ends).
2 T unsalted butter
2 T sliced or chopped almonds, toasted
kosher salt and pepper

Directions:

1. Wash and trim green beans.
2. Place in a vegetable steamer over 2 inches of water in a large saucepan. Steam beans over medium-high heat for 5 minutes, or until crisp-tender with a fork.
3. Drain and toss with butter, almonds, salt and pepper.

Profiteroles

Cream Puffs…easy and great to freeze for an anytime dessert. If you have time, consider making a vanilla cream filling and top the puff with a chocolate glaze, which is more traditional. This recipe is prepared with ice cream and a drizzle of homemade chocolate sauce. Use purchased chocolate sauce to save time.

Serves: 4-5

Ingredients:
- ¼ cup water
- ¼ cup milk
- ¼ cup butter
- ¼ tsp sugar
- ⅛ tsp salt
- ½ cup flour
- 3 eggs

Directions:

1. Preheat oven 425 degrees F and grease a baking sheet or use parchment paper.
2. In a 2qt saucepan, bring the first 5 ingredients to a full boil (water, milk, butter, sugar, salt).
3. Remove from heat, add the flour and put back on heat. Stir rigorously with a wooden spoon until the dough is removed completely from the sides and forms a ball. Remove from heat.
4. Add eggs one at a time, stirring vigorously until all shininess of each egg disappears.
5. Place roughly ½ cup dough onto baking sheet at least 3 inches apart (they double in size).
6. Bake approximately 30 min or until golden brown. Don't remove too soon or they will collapse.

Chocolate Sauce

Ingredients:
½ cup semi-sweet dark chocolate bits
2T milk or half & half
2 tsp cognac or coffee (leftover from morning is fine, flavored coffee works well too)

Directions:

1. In a small saucepan, melt the chocolate over low heat.
2. Add the milk and cognac or coffee, butter and vanilla and stir until smooth. If too thick, add more milk.

Assemble:
I like to reheat the shells before serving in a 350 degree oven for a few minutes. Split the puffs in half with a sharp knife. Fill with your favorite ice cream (French vanilla, but any favorite is fine) and drizzle with the hot chocolate sauce. Sprinkle with nuts if you like. Serve immediately.

Extra notes:
To the one who prepares dinner . . . no one eats until you say 'Bon appétit.' The French way of eating is to use your fork in the left hand and the knife in the right.

Film D'Amour

Consider ending your evening wrapped up in the arms of your lover and watching one of these movies with a French theme:

Les Misérables
Phantom of the Opera
Amélie
Chocolat
An American in Paris
Sabrina
French Kiss
Da Vinci Code
Midnight in Paris

French Phrases to use throughout the evening:

Je t'aime . . . I love you
L'amour de ma vie . . . Love of my life
S'il vous plait . . . If it pleases you!

Making Great Memories

Valentine's Day with a French Twist Toolbox

Many of the following items can be found at:
www.makinggreatmemories.com/shop/

Laguiole Knife
Picnic basket
Parisian table setting
The French Look (model after Audrey Hepburn)
Red satin sheets
Bed net
Red light bulb
Adult toys
Parisian bedroom costume

Valentine's Day with a French Twist video @
http://www.makinggreatmemories.com/videos

Notes & Memories

3

Spring Into Love With Golf

Introduction

Spring signifies coming out of hibernation and the opportunity for rebirth. When the sun grows warm and everything turns green, it's finally time to play golf! Although my family is of Scottish descent, and the game of golf originated in Scotland, I haven't always been a golf fan; as I've grown in maturity so has my love for the game. The majority of golfers are male, but I'm eager for women to catch on to the secret that men seem to have been keeping for years.

Here are the essential elements of the game that women may not know: Golf is about finesse and not strength. Golf is a social sport and provides the opportunity to network and possibly boost your career. It's played in some of the most beautiful places in the world, and the sport's fashion is great – think cute, comfortable and classy. Lastly, cocktails and conversation are always waiting at the 19th hole. A great way for newcomers to learn the game is to start with golf classes designed just for rookies, or with women in mind. Wine and Nine or Golf Fore Women classes are fun and challenging and, of course, you're more likely to improve and stay with the game once you've invested your time in classes.

I think it's also important to understand that golf is one of the few games in which men and women compete equally. Because golf has a handicap system, in which ladies play with forward tees, it means we often land our drives in the same place as men do. This system allows couples to play side-by-side and share a healthy, fun hobby together. Unfortunately, there are still golf courses in our country that don't allow women to play, including the Augusta National, home of the Masters. I realize there are places and times when men just want to goof around, just as there are times we just want to be silly with our girlfriends without any significant-others around. On the golf course, men tend to want to be free to smoke cigars, make crude jokes, or keep up a masculine banter – especially because there's so much walking and waiting involved in the game.

Men – invite your ladies! We are the key to the next generation of golfers and we typically control the money and time in our families, so seriously consider making golf a couples activity. Ladies, if you're single and looking for love, consider picking up the game. The odds are high: 80% of golfers are men, and it's a sport that caters to socialization and getting to know new people. Plus, men tend to find female golfers very attractive.

This *Making Great Memories* golf theme is perfect for many different occasions, including a special birthday or Father's Day. Any occasion in the spring is also timely, because the Masters is in April and the buzz, excitement and discussion of winners and losers continues long afterward. If you're planning this theme as a birthday celebration, or perhaps for Father's Day, consider buying your partner tickets to a PGA tour. They are relatively inexpensive, occur all over the country, and are incredibly exciting to witness live rather than on television. There's a lot of etiquette expected at these events, so make sure you've reviewed the expectations ahead of time. You could also take him to experience TopGolf. TopGolf is a sports entertainment facility that's as much about the food, music, drinking, and socializing as it is about golf. They're popping up all over the country, and you don't need to be a golfer to enjoy the experience. You could also purchase a set of custom golf balls with his picture on them. It's been my experience that men like to show off their game balls!

Let's Get This Par-Tee Started!

The final day of the Masters tends to be the first day of the season for my partner and me to play golf. Following our first outing, I usually plan a 19th hole cocktail hour at home, which we enjoy while watching the final round of The Masters. Set a cocktail table with a green tablecloth, and, though tacky, embellish it with golf napkins, plates, and use golf tees for toothpicks. Drink Arnold Palmers or John Daly's and eat food traditionally from Georgia, or the concession-style eats spectators enjoy at the Masters. Recipes to follow.

Dress Fore Play

If you want to knock his argyle socks off, go to my website, www.makinggreatmemories.com/shop/ where I provide a link to purchase the Kilted Scottie Hottie costume. There's even a Scottish costume for men.

Check out John Daly's outfits online and dare your partner to find a pair of pants and dress like him. Or maybe you can talk him into wearing a pair of knickers and argyle socks like Payne Stewart. He may not be up for either, but encourage him by telling him how sexy you'll find his outfit. If you prefer, a sweet gesture would be to buy him a new golf shirt.

Music and Comedy

While sipping on your Arnold Palmer, you and your partner need to find a screen and watch and listen to the following golf songs and videos. They are Caddyshack funny.

"The Masters" Theme Song

"Straight Down the Middle" by Bing Crosby

"Hit It Hard" by John Daly

"Bohemian Rhapsody" - A golfing parody Tribute by Nigel Tait

"Love the One You Whiff" by Jake Trout and the Flounders

"Stone Cold Pro" by Gus Van Sant

And finally, if you've never watched Robin Williams stand up golf routine on YouTube, NOW is the time! (Warning it does contain strong language, but the funniest comedy skit on golf you will ever see.)

The Menu

The Spring into Love menu is inspired by traditional foods sold at the concession stands at The Masters, with a Southern twist. To keep it simple, serve egg salad sandwiches and chips. If y'all are inspired to "up your game," research recipes from our favorite Southern gal, Paula Deen.

A Southern-Inspired Master's Menu

Arnold Palmer Cocktail and Mocktail
Pimento Cheese Sandwiches with Fried Green Tomatoes served on a Southern Buttermilk Biscuit
Black-Eyed Pea Salad for good luck
Georgia Peach Ice Cream Sandwich

Recipes:

Arnold Palmer

This is a traditional 19th hole favorite (half iced tea, half lemonade) *made with or without alcohol that is very refreshing. To make a John Daly, omit the bourbon and use vodka.*

Serves: Makes a pitcher

Ingredients:
- 5 tea bags
- ¾ cup sugar
- 1 tsp lemon zest
- 1 cup bourbon
- ½ cup fresh lemon juice

Directions:

Bring 4 C water to a boil and steep 5 tea bags, ¾ C sugar, 1 tsp lemon zest for 5 min.

Strain into a pitcher and add 4 C cold water, 1 C Bourbon, ½ C fresh lemon juice. Chill. Delicious even without the bourbon.

Pimento Cheese Spread with Fried Green Tomatoes and Buttermilk Biscuits

It doesn't get more Southern than this!

Serves: Makes 3 Cups

Ingredients:
- 1 8oz package of shredded yellow cheddar cheese
- 1 8oz package of white shredded cheddar cheese
- 1 (4 oz) jar red pimentos with the juice or ½ Cup fire roasted red peppers
- ½ cup mayonnaise
- Salt and pepper to taste

Directions:

Mix all the ingredients together and refrigerate. Use in sandwiches, deviled eggs or with corn chips.

Fried Green Tomatoes

Serves 4

Ingredients:
- 2 firm green tomatoes
- 1 egg
- 3 T milk (or buttermilk)
- ½ tsp kosher salt
- ¼ tsp fresh black pepper
- 3/4 cup flour
- ¼ cup cracker crumbs or cornmeal
- 1 cup vegetable oil for frying

Directions:

1. Wash and slice tomatoes into ¼ inch slices.
2. In one bowl, beat egg with milk, salt and pepper.
3. In another bowl, combine flour and cracker crumbs.
4. Dip the tomatoes into the egg mixture, then the crumbs and fry in oil that is at 350 degrees. Cook the tomatoes for 6 minutes, flipping half way. Drain on paper towel.

Southern Buttermilk Biscuits

Makes 10-12 biscuits

Ingredients:
- 2 cups flour
- 1 T baking powder
- ½ tsp salt
- ½ tsp baking soda
- ½ cup vegetable shortening
- 1 cup buttermilk

Directions:

1. Combine the dry ingredients in a medium bowl.
2. Cut in the shortening with a fork or pastry blender.
3. Blend in the buttermilk, then turn dough onto a floured counter and mix very gently to combine all ingredients. Do not overmix!
4. Roll out into 1 inch thickness and cut with a 2 or 3 inch biscuit cutter.
5. Bake in a preheated oven at 450 degrees F for 12-15 minutes depending on size of biscuit.
6. To assemble the Master's Inspired Southern Style Pimento Sandwich, split the buttermilk biscuit and spread a layer of pimento on both sides of the biscuit. Top with fried green tomato.
   Suggestion: Adding two slices of crisp bacon to the sandwich takes it to a whole new level of yum.

Black Eyed Pea Salad

A true Southern tradition!

Serves: 3-4

Ingredients:
- 2 T vinegar
- 1 T olive oil
- 1 T sugar
- Dash salt and pepper
- 2 cups canned black eyed peas, drained
- ½ cup celery, diced
- 2 T cilantro, chopped
- ¼ cup red pepper, diced
- ¼ green pepper, diced
- ¼ onion, diced

Directions:

1. Mix together the first 4 ingredients, then add the rest, combining thoroughly.
2. Cover and chill for at least 2 hours.

Simple Georgia Peach Ice Cream Sandwiches

Ingredients:
- Sugar cookies
- Peach ice cream
- Toasted pecans (optional)

Directions:
Purchase sugar cookies or make your favorite sugar cookie recipe. Let the peach ice cream soften enough to spread between 2 cookies. Roll the sides of the cookies into toasted chopped pecans. Serve immediately.

Final Round Cuddle Time

After the final round of the Master's and the "Green Jacket" ceremony, consider these golf-themed movie classics:

Caddyshack
Tin Cup
The Legend of Bagger Vance
Happy Gilmore
The Greatest Game Ever Played

Making Great Memories

GOLF Toolbox

Many of the following items can be found at:
www.makinggreatmemories.com/shop/

Golf inspired tableware: green napkins, golf plates, green tablecloth, etc.
Gift suggestions: PGA tickets, custom golf balls, golf shirt
The Kilted Scottie Hottie

Notes & Memories

4

Frugal Fun Friday

Introduction:

It's easy to complain about politics or work, but really, how lucky are we to live in this country? Most of us grow up with a free education, an opportunity for a secondary school, enjoy good health care and live with the right to freely express ourselves. We live in warm homes with warm meals every day.

The inspiration for this theme came after much self-reflection and mediation on all that I have to be grateful for in my life. I have plenty of opportunities to spend money more thoughtfully (and less impulsively) and I encourage you to consider engaging in the same self-reflection. Being mindful of how you are spending money is the first step to saving money. Stop yourself from making unnecessary purchases, and instead use money to be generous to others. Consider using these resources to make charitable donations or support a neighbor in need.

Frugal Fun Friday is one of my favorite and most personal theme ideas. I like it so much that I've repeated it a few times. It can easily be adapted as a challenge with a friend or significant other. I challenged myself to create an entire date night for under forty dollars, including everything: the table settings, the outfit, the food and the entertainment! I love to shop at thrift stores, flea markets, garage sales and yes, The Dollar Store. I admit it's a hobby of mine to hunt down a bargain, whether food, clothing, entertainment, or home decor. Even if I had millions of dollars, I believe I would still live frugally. I hate waste and find it irresponsible not to recycle and reuse. Giving away gently-used items to churches and nonprofits is a great way to clean out your house and help others. I never pay full price for anything, because, with a little patience, the price always goes down. A real trick is to ask yourself, before every purchase, "Do I need this item, or can I live without it?" I spent the first half of my life acquiring stuff and the second half of my life getting rid of it, and I know I'm not the only one my age who has gone through this process. Honestly, I love that life is now more about making memories than about having things. Millennials have quickly become known for being a generation more concerned with having experiences than with acquiring stuff. That's smart.

I'm going to outline how I put this evening together, and I'm also going to add a few suggestions to help spark your imagination. For my challenge, I gave myself one afternoon to pull it all together. This is because it's one of my personality quirks that I work best under a time constraint and have the ability to conquer great feats under pressure. Take a week to put this all together if that works for you; just enjoy and have some frugal fun.

Setting up for Frugal Fun

Let your partner know you are planning a Frugal Fun Friday. Together you can decide on how much money you are going to allow for this evening. Remember, keeping it frugal and challenging makes it a lot more fun.

Creating the atmosphere was my favorite part of the challenge. I loved going on a search for the table setting. I was looking for two dinner plates (something a little unusual), martini glasses and dessert dishes. I also found two placemats, beautiful linen napkins, and a candle holder. Almost every item was $1.00 or less. A tablecloth, vase, salt and pepper shakers, wine or water glasses, cordial glasses, a pitcher, and salad or dessert plates are other items that might add a touch of frugal elegance to your table setting.

Another absolute must for the table are flowers, and free is my favorite flower. I have flowers in my yard, but I also love pulling over and picking some right from the side of the road if I see a particularly lovely bunch. Other fun and free adventures are to step into the woods or a park and forage for rare ferns and twigs. If you look closely, you can find local flora with many unique and natural touches. In the winter, I love to search for forsythia stems or apple tree branches. I did this challenge in January, in Savannah, Georgia, and I picked up a beautiful Camellia flower from the ground while strolling through the city's beautiful squares. I floated the flower in a shallow glass dish lined with seashells I had collected from the shores of Tybee Island.

Frugal Music

If you haven't already downloaded a free music app for your laptop, phone or tablet (such as Pandora or Spotify) you seriously need to do it! These music apps have so many genres that you can customize to your liking; and, if you have wireless speakers, you can listen to it all over your house. You can also stream music through your cable television.

The Frugal Outfit

I've been a Goodwill shopper all my life; yes, even before it was cool to shop there. People don't always realize that new clothing often hangs on the racks as well as old. For this theme, I purchased a Calvin Klein knit dress (which ordinarily sells over $80.00) for only $4.99! Even better, many communities have thrift stores that support The Humane Society, recovery centers, and churches. I also like shopping at the Salvation Army or, for a most unusual experience, a Goodwill store where you pay by the pound.

Frugal Fun

While on my frugal shopping expedition, I came across the card game "Battle of the Sexes" for only $2.00. You can find lots of board games, puzzles, and odd books and movies at second-hand shops. We played "Battle of the Sexes" while drinking our Sangria and roasting the chicken. Strolling around the neighborhood after dinner, or attending a free concert in the park are also excellent and inexpensive ways to end an evening. Sunsets are free too! And if you can't afford the theater, Netflix or Redbox are great, low cost alternatives.

Frugal-Inspired Meal

I find that the perfect frugal meal is one that can be used to create additional meals. My favorite frugal meal begins with roasting a big chicken. Once you eat the first meal of roast chicken, you can then make chicken salad or a casserole; and finally, the third meal can be a chicken soup made from the carcass. Try timing a frugal meal after Thanksgiving to get discounted turkeys. You can also find great discounts on large pork loins to cut into smaller portions to save money. And whatever you don't use, throw in the freezer for later!

I often make suggestions to use the grocery store for pre-made items to save time and for convenience on date nights—but not for this theme. Anyone who lives frugally loves being resourceful and has acquired a lot of skill in doing so. It forces you to set your priorities and learn how to live on a budget, how to create healthy menus (can't afford to get sick), and how to grocery shop. Frugal people know their communities well, so that they can compare prices, and they enjoy learning cooking skills, to avoid eating out. These are the recipes I used for one of my Frugal Fun Fridays, but if you want to explore other recipes and keep with the theme, consider cookbooks by The Frugal Gourmet or Chef On A Shoestring.

The Frugal Inspired Menu

Spanish Sangria Pitcher
Homemade Hummus
Romaine Salad with Feta and Orange served with Homemade Dressings
One-Pot Bacon Top Roast Chicken and Vegetables
Easy Homemade Chocolate Pudding
Additional Recipes:
Mom's Homemade Chicken Soup
Allie's Chicken Salad
Homemade Cordials

Recipes:

Spanish Sangria

Sangria is an excellent choice for this frugal concept because it's super cheap to make at home but still has a beautiful and colorful presentation. Make it ahead of time so the fruit can ferment, and nobody will know you used a $3.00 bottle of wine for the base. You can also create a nonalcoholic version with sparkling cider. Either way, serve it in a beautiful pitcher. For the fruit, look for the discount cart at the grocery store and stock up — you can put any extra in the freezer and use later for cooking, and making smoothies.

Serves: Makes a pitcher

Ingredients:

- 1 bottle red wine (cheap is fine)
- 1/3 cup white sugar
- 1 Granny Smith apple sliced
- 1 peach sliced
- 1 lemon sliced
- 1 lime sliced
- 1 cinnamon stick, crushed a little
- 1 bottle lemon/lime carbonated soda

Directions:

1. In a large pitcher, combine all ingredients except the soda and refrigerate for at least an hour, preferably overnight.
2. Just before serving, add the lemon/lime soda and serve in a wine glass, including the fruit.

Hummus

A favorite frugal appetizer is a homemade hummus. Once you purchase the tahini, you can make many batches of hummus for a fraction of the price you pay in grocery stores. To go along with the hummus, try making your own toasted and flavored pita chips. I frequently shop the day-old bread stores (the food is still tasty, especially if you'll be toasting it) and add my favorite flavor combinations. Many day-old bakeries sell their items practically free, and the freezer is a great place to store the bread, bagels, English muffins, buns and pita pockets.

Serves: Makes 1 ½ Cups

Ingredients:
- 2 (15 oz) cans of chickpeas, drain only one of them
- 1 lemon, juiced
- ½ cup tahini
- 3 cloves of garlic, crushed
- kosher salt and fresh ground pepper to taste

Directions:
Place all the ingredients into a food processor or blender and mix until smooth. Spoon into a bowl and cover lightly with olive oil and paprika or parsley. Variations: Add a small jar of roasted red peppers (drained) or caramelized onions.

Romaine Salad with Feta and Orange

Buy a head of romaine lettuce and wash it by hand or with a salad spinner. This is much more economical than paying for the pre-washed lettuce. Add an orange, some feta cheese from the Dollar Store, and make your salad dressing at home to save even more money. I have three simple homemade dressings that I love to prepare. Place all the ingredients in a recycled jar and shake before serving:

Lemon/shallot Vinaigrette

¼ cup olive oil, ¼ cup fresh lemon juice, 2 tsp honey, 1 minced shallot, salt and pepper

Balsamic/Dijon Vinaigrette

⅓ cup olive oil, 3 T balsamic vinegar, 2 tsp dijon mustard, salt and pepper

Creamy Parmesan Dressing

½ cup olive oil, ½ cup parmesan cheese, ¼ cup sour cream, 2 T white wine vinegar, salt and pepper

One-Pot Bacon Top Roast Chicken with Vegetables

It doesn't get any easier than a one-pot meal, and the smell in your kitchen will be divine. Make the leftover chicken into chicken salad, and, finally, use the remaining carcass for the stock in a family chicken soup.

Serves: 2-4 with leftovers

Ingredients:
- 1 lb red potatoes, cut into large chunks
- 1 large onion, large slices
- 1 large sweet potato, cut into large chunks
- 2 large carrots peeled, cut into large pieces
- 3 T olive oil, 1 tsp kosher salt and ½ tsp fresh ground black pepper
- 3 cloves of garlic, crushed
- 1 tsp dried oregano
- 1 tsp dried rosemary
- ½ tsp fresh ground pepper
- 2 T butter, softened
- 2 slices of thick, smoked applewood bacon
- 1 (4-5 pound) whole roasting chicken

Directions:
1. Mix ingredients in a large bowl (the potatoes, onion, sweet potato and carrots). Toss with olive oil, salt and pepper.
2. Discard giblets and neck from chicken. Rinse chicken under cold water, then pat dry. Truss the chicken and place in roasting pan. Rub the softened butter all over the chicken. Place cloves of garlic in the cavity of the chicken. Sprinkle the herbs inside and outside of chicken. Sprinkle with black pepper. Lay the bacon crisscrossing over the chicken. Place vegetables all around the chicken.

3. Roast in 375 degree F oven about 1 hour and 15 minutes, or until the meat thermometer registers 180 degrees F. Stir the vegetables occasionally. Remove from oven, let stand for 10 minutes before carving. Serve with roasted vegetables.

Easy Homemade Chocolate Pudding

I found the perfect portions of chocolate chip morsels and a pint of milk at The Dollar Store that, when combined with a few simple ingredients, became a delicious chocolate pudding. The Dollar Store also had the whipped cream!

Serves: 2

Ingredients:
- 2 T sugar
- 1 T cornstarch
- 1 cup milk
- ⅓ cup semisweet chocolate chips
- ½ tsp vanilla

Directions:

1. In a small saucepan, combine the sugar and cornstarch. Add milk, stir until smooth.
2. Cook and stir over medium heat until mixture comes to a boil. Cook 2 more minutes until thick.
3. Stir in the chocolate chips until melted. Remove from heat and add the vanilla.
4. Spoon into dessert dishes and serve warm or cold with whipped cream.

Additional Recipes:

Chicken Stock

*Once you have removed most of the meat from the chicken, place the carcass in a large stockpot and fill with water. Add celery leaves and stalk, carrot peelings and onion slices, salt and pepper. Bring to a boil, turn off burner and let it sit for an hour. Strain and use for soup or place in recycled containers (large yogurt containers work well) and freeze for future use.

Mom's Homemade Chicken Soup

Giving away your money isn't the only way to be a generous person. Giving your time along with a thoughtful gesture is also incredibly noble. I love chicken soup, especially my mom's. I've included her recipe (exactly as written by Mom) that has become a staple regularly in my freezer. Always there to comfort a cold for a family member or to comfort a neighbor in time of need. Nothing warms the heart like chicken soup, so consider making a big batch and storing it in recycled containers in your freezer.

Makes: 10 Cups

Ingredients:
- 10 cups chicken stock
- 1 large onion chopped
- 4 celery ribs chopped
- 6 carrots sliced
- ½ cup frozen peas
- 1 cup orzo (or other small pasta)
- ¼ cup barley
- 1 T Gravy Master or soy sauce
- 1 T dried parsley
- 3 Bay leaves
- Salt and pepper to taste
- 2 cups cooked chicken

Directions:
Heat the stock, then add the onions, celery and carrots. Bring to a boil and add the pasta and barley. Add the seasonings. Cook on medium until the barley is done (15-20 minutes). Add the frozen peas and cooked chicken, then simmer another 10 minutes. Remove bay leaves before serving.

Allie's Chicken Salad

One of my favorite traits about my daughter Allie, when she was growing up, was her love of food. It isn't often you see a little girl rip through a lobster or devour the leaves of an artichoke! Allie always had the most unusual food in her lunch box. Curry chicken salad is one of her favorites.

Serves: 4 Servings

Ingredients:

    ½ cup sliced almonds (toasted)
    2 cups cooked chicken
    3/4 cup seedless red or green grapes, halved or dried cranberries
    1 large celery rib, chopped
    3/4 cup mayonnaise
    1 T honey
    1 tsp curry powder
    Kosher salt and fresh ground pepper to taste

Directions:

1. Toast the almonds (small frying pan on medium heat until golden, cool)
2. In a large bowl, combine the almonds, chicken, grapes and celery.
3. Add the mayonnaise, honey, curry powder, salt and pepper. Mix well and refrigerate until ready to serve.
4. Serve on bread of choice or in lettuce or radicchio cups. Also good on crackers.

Frugal and Fun Homemade Cordials

A great frugal gift for friends and family is homemade liquors. I've included in this theme recipes for homemade Raspberry Cordial, Coffee Liqueur, and Irish Cream. Find beautiful bottles at tag sales or Goodwill, and give these cordials as hostess gifts or Christmas presents.

Raspberry Cordial

My family loves the tradition of picking berries. Some of the best conversations with my children happened in a berry patch. Forging for food is a wonderful way to save money and berries keep well in the freezer.

Ingredients:
- 2 cups sugar
- 2 pints raspberries
- 1 quart vodka

Directions:
Place sugar in a 3 quart glass container with a lid. Add fruit and vodka. Cover and place in a cool, dark place. Each week for 2 months, open and stir. Strain using coffee filters when it gets cloudy. Pour into various glass containers. Store in a cool place.

Homemade Coffee Liqueur

Ingredients:
- 4 cups water
- 4 cups sugar
- 2 ½ tsp vanilla
- 4 T instant coffee
- Fifth of vodka

Directions:

Boil 3 cups water and 4 cups sugar for 20 minutes. Add vanilla and let cool. Dissolve coffee in remaining 1 Cup of water. Add to syrup. When cold, add the vodka and store in a glass container. Let sit for at least 2 weeks. Store in a cool place.

Homemade Irish Cream Liqueur

Ingredients:
- 1 ¾ cup Irish whiskey or brandy, rum, scotch or bourbon
- 1 14 oz condensed milk (sweetened)
- 2 cups whipping cream
- 2 T chocolate syrup
- 2 tsp instant coffee
- 1 tsp vanilla extract
- ½ tsp almond extract

Directions:
Combine all the ingredients in a blender. Store tightly covered in the refrigerator up to 3 weeks.

Cuddle Time

End your Frugal Fun Friday cuddling with your sweetie and watching one of these movies about living with limited means:

Robin Hood
Pursuit of Happiness
Slumdog Millionaire
Trading Places
It's a Wonderful Life
The Game
Dirty Dancing
Indecent Proposal

Did I accomplish my goal of $40.00?

    2 dinner plates = $2.00
    2 cool martini glasses = $2.00
    2 glass dessert cups = $2.00
    2 placemats = $2.00
    2 linen napkins = $2.00
    1 candle holder = $1.00
    1 bouquet flowers = free
    1 Dress = $4.99
    1 board game "Battle of the Sexes" = $2.00
    1 bottle of Two Buck Chuck from Trader Joe's = $2.99
    1 bottle soda = $1.00
    apple, peach, lemon and lime = $1.50
    chickpeas for the hummus = 89¢
    tahini (4.99 container) = 50¢
    pita bread = 36¢
    4-5lb chicken (on sale) = $7.00
    2 thick slices applewood smoked bacon = $1.75
    roasting vegetables = $2.50

chocolate chips 3 oz = $1.00
pint milk = $1.00
Can whipped cream = $1.00

Total: $39.48

I did it! So now I'll return to Goodwill, buy a piggy bank, and start saving for the next Frugal Fun Friday!

Making Great Memories

Frugal Fun Toolbox

Inexpensive table settings
Free flowers
Inexpensive outfit
Fun game
Glass bottles for cordial gifts
Pretty pitcher

Notes & Memories

Notes & Memories

5

When A Man Loves A Woman (Man Plan)

Introduction

Balancing work and home life is incredibly exhausting, especially when you're trying to raise a family and keep your marriage a priority. When I think back to just starting out in my twenties, there's a lot I wish I had known. I'm sure my parents offered advice, but I was too stubborn to listen at the time. It seems that society pressures young women into thinking a career is most important, so we often don't spend enough time on our personal happiness. I believe spiritual commitment needs to come first in life and then all things are possible. You also need to love yourself and practice that love. That means making time for exercise, eating healthy, getting enough rest, and not letting things like social media take up your valuable time. Keep your life balanced. As I've mentioned in other themes, our time is one of our most precious assets, and just as it's the most important gift we can give to our sweethearts, it's the most important one we can give ourselves too.

Finally, you need to make time for relationships. Be present with the people you love and allow others to be there for you. Don't give the impression you are Super Woman and you can do it all, because no one person can do everything. Trying to do so will inevitably lead to loneliness and regrets at the time misspent. When you are in a committed relationship, make it a priority.

This theme night was created for a gentleman to use to make a great memory for that special woman in his life. Careful consideration goes into the planning around time, costs, and skill. I guarantee you will both enjoy this so much that you'll want to do it again. Ladies, no matter what your partner plans for this evening, avoid being critical. It's unlikely he'll do things the way you would, but that's why there are two people in a relationship – we excite and stimulate one another with our quirks. Recognize that he's doing this because, quite simply, he loves you. All of his plans for the evening come from that place of love, so skip the criticism – even if you think you're making a joke. If he senses he's being ridiculed or judged, he probably won't be too excited about doing something special again, and, quite frankly, who can blame him?

We all love to be admired by our partners, and men are no different! If you want to get the most out of this night and build long-lasting intimacy, make sure he knows how much you appreciate him.

Girls, please don't read any further! You will enjoy this theme I promise, but don't spoil all the surprises. Just make sure your guy sees this theme and enjoy the anticipation.

Homework for the week:

Men, let her know in advance that you have a special evening planned for her. You want to show her how much you appreciate all that she does, so plan to do this on a Friday night after work. If you tell her at the beginning of the week, she'll love the anticipation. You'll need to arrive home before she does, so plan accordingly.

In preparation, consider reading *The 5 Love Languages* by Gary Chapman. It's an informative book that will help you to better understand not only your partner but also yourself, especially how you function within a relationship. It's short and sweet and, I promise, your relationship will never be the same—it will only get better.

Creating the Mood:

The moment your girl walks through the door, escort her to the sofa, take off her shoes and rub her feet. Tell her that you'll need a little time getting the evening prepared, so suggest she relax with a bath and then put on something pretty. Tell her exactly what time to reappear – perhaps an hour – and no sooner. If you send her off with *The 5 Love Languages* book, she'll be touched by your thoughtfulness. When she's settled into the bath, surprise her with a glass of wine and maybe a candle. Wear a nice pair of pants with a collared shirt, and keep in mind that there are few things sexier than a handsome man in an apron. If you want to add extra playfulness to your evening, refer to my website www.makinggreatmemories.com/shop/ to shop for unusual and sexy aprons.

You'll need to create three spaces. The first is for the cocktail and appetizer. Consider setting up your space in the living room, using a coffee table, or perhaps out on a deck. Set out a placemat with a votive candle and a small bouquet of flowers. Both can be purchased at a grocery store to save time running around. It is fine to cut down the bouquet of flowers into two or three small vases to be used in all three settings. Use a clean mason jar or drinking glass if you don't have a vase.

The second space will be your dining room table and here's where you're going to impress your sweetheart. You need to set the table correctly and who better to guide you than the experts at the Emily Post Institute using their Table Setting Guide. They also offer advice on table manners, which we all could use a refresher on once in awhile. Set the table ahead of time. If you have dishes you only use for special occasions, tonight is a splendid time to pull them out, along with a lovely tablecloth and set of linen napkins. Place candles and flowers atop the tablecloth and dim the lights to create a romantic mood.

The last space will be the bedroom. Pull down the bed covers and put a rose on the bed, and maybe a few chocolates, just as if you're at a nice hotel with a turndown service. This touch will send a subtle message to your girl when she steps into the bedroom. If your bouquet of flowers has a rose in it, you can take the petals off and make a heart on the bed. Play soft music in the background and make sure the lighting is low. Don't set it too low, though, because you want to be able to see and admire one another. We are visual creatures, and there's no reason why we shouldn't celebrate each other's bodies with appropriate lighting. It feels so good to know your partner wants to see all of you.

Healthy relationships need intimacy, and of course, physical closeness is a foundation of that intimacy. It's exciting and important to allow our partners to see and admire us in nothing more than our birthday suits. I understand taking issue with certain parts of our body; I've spent a lifetime trying to plump up certain places and slim down others. I also understand that men have physical insecurities too. What I've learned though, is that men – and women – are most attracted to a partner who is confident, comfortable in their skin and open about their sexuality. Most importantly, we want to know that our partner finds us desirable. An entirely dark room just can't happen, and shouldn't happen, because we need to see one another to express that desire and explore new levels of intimacy. This intimacy is so important, and we need to commit to a lifetime of letting one another know how sexy we find one another, and how lucky we are to share a life together.

Music:

Music certainly sets the mood in this theme and should be placed in each setting. Play music you know she will love; maybe from the decade you first met, or love songs from various genres. You can never go wrong with jazz. Play the music at a volume that you can easily hear but still have a conversation because one thing your woman truly appreciates is your focused attention.

Couple Time Together:

If you want to make this evening memorable, this element is imperative. Just as men love feeling admired and respected for their job and for supporting their family, women need to feel appreciated for all they do, and know that they are desirable to their man. So tonight, over your appetizer and during dinner, don't just tell her she's beautiful, tell her specifically what you find attractive. Her eyes? Her laugh? Her ambition? If you have children, tell her why she's a good mother. Talk about the future together, or even plan a vacation or a weekend getaway. Create a list of things you want to do together in the future – a couple's Bucket List! Tell her she smells good, touch her skin softly, look deeply into her eyes. Be entirely present. If you want to have a little silliness, consider filling in Mad Libs together. Mad Libs in Love is one of my favorites.

A Dinner To Impress Her:

Simply put, a woman likes a man who can cook. It need not be complicated or expensive, just keep it simple and relaxed. Men often struggle with the idea of planning an entire meal, but careful consideration has gone into this menu, which will boost your confidence and delight your date. If you want to stretch your culinary skills, consider preparing recipes from celebrity chefs like Tyler Florence, Bobby Flay, and Emeril Lagasse.

When A Man Loves A Woman The Menu

Specialty Cocktail of your choice or wine
Red Pepper Hummus with Vegetables and Crackers
Caesar Salad or Chopped Salad
Pan-Seared Salmon with Roasted Vegetables over Rice Pilaf
Or
New York Strip Steak with Herb Butter and Oven Baked Potatoes
So-Easy Chocolate Cream Pie

Cocktail:

Women do love a man who can make a good cocktail, so if you have a specialty, or something new you'd like to try, go for it. Otherwise, red wine is good for the heart. Pinot Noir slightly chilled would be nice too. A fine, nonalcoholic choice; sparkling water with a slice of lemon served in a pretty glass.

Appetizer:

Red Pepper Hummus with Vegetables and Crackers

We're aiming for impressive and uncomplicated. Purchase a container of red pepper hummus from your favorite grocery store. If your grocer has a salad and/or olive bar, gather sliced cucumbers, carrots, celery, or any type of vegetable you both enjoy. Add pitted black olives, feta cheese, and warmed naan bread or favorite crackers. Place everything on a pretty platter or plate.

Caesar Salad or Chopped Salad

Buy the pre-made package in the produce section, and mix it up just before serving. Use a salad bowl and tongs.

Dinner for Two: Option #1

Pan-Seared Salmon with Oven-Roasted Vegetables served over Rice Pilaf

Simple, colorful, healthy and delicious, you can't go wrong with this dinner menu! Many produce sections have pre-made packages of cut-up vegetables ready to go to save time.

Serves 2

Ingredients:
- 1 box rice pilaf or pre-made package for quick preparation
- 1 cup broccoli florets
- 1 yellow squash, sliced and quartered
- 1 zucchini squash, sliced and quartered
- 1 small red pepper, chopped
- 1 small red onion, chopped
- 1 cup crimini or button mushrooms
- 1 T olive oil
- 1 T balsamic vinegar (optional)
- 2 cloves garlic, minced (optional)
- ½ tsp Italian seasoning (optional)
- kosher salt and fresh ground pepper to taste
- 1 lemon
- 2T olive oil
- 2 (6-8 oz) salmon fillets, skin removed

Directions:

1. If using boxed rice pilaf, follow directions on package.
2. Preheat oven to 425 degrees F. Wash and cut the vegetables and place in a single layer on a baking sheet.
3. In a small bowl, mix together the 1T olive oil, balsamic, garlic, Italian seasoning, and salt and pepper. Pour over vegetables and toss gently. Vegetables can be roasted with just olive oil and salt and pepper if you don't have the other ingredients. Place into oven and bake 12-15 minutes or until tender.
4. While the vegetables are cooking, preheat a cast iron skillet (or heavy frying pan) over medium heat. Season the salmon fillets with kosher salt and fresh ground pepper.
5. Add 2 T of oil to the skillet, followed by the salmon; cook for 3-4 minutes. Squeeze the juice from half a lemon over the tops of the fillets; flip.
6. Cook the fillets 2-3 more minutes until the fish flakes easily or internal temperature is 135 degrees F. Remove from burner, squeeze remaining lemon over salmon, cover and rest a few minutes while plating the rest of the dinner.
7. Plate your dish with the vegetables, rice and the salmon fillet accompanied by a wedge of lemon.

Option #2

New York Strip Steaks with Oven Baked Potatoes

This meal is a re-creation of the first meal my husband ever prepared for me. It remains his "go to" dinner and is always done to perfection!

Serves 2

Ingredients:

    2 large Russet potatoes washed thoroughly
    olive oil
    Salt and pepper
    2 (8-10 oz) New York Strip Steaks, leave out in room temperature for 20 minutes before grilling
    Dry steak seasoning
    ½ stick (4 T) unsalted butter
    1 tsp fresh minced parsley
    1 clove garlic minced
    1 small pinch dry steak seasoning of your choice

Directions:

1. Prepare the herb butter by placing the butter, parsley, garlic and dry steak seasoning into a small bowl. Mix well to combine, then put it on a piece of plastic wrap and roll up into a log. Refrigerate.
2. Preheat oven to 425 degrees F.
3. Wash potatoes and rub with olive oil. Sprinkle with salt and pepper. Prick potatoes with a fork and lay them directly on the oven rack of your preheated oven. Cook the potatoes for 1 hour until their skins are crispy and can be pricked easily with a fork.
4. Preheat the grill over medium heat.

5. Season the steak liberally with the dry steak seasoning or just with kosher salt and pepper. Add steaks to grill over direct heat. Cover and cook, undisturbed, for 4-5 minutes. (My hubby always uses a timer, which is why he probably always cooks steaks to perfection.) Flip steaks and move to indirect heat until internal temperature is 135 degrees F for medium rare/medium, about 3-4 more minutes depending on the cut. Remove from grill and let rest about 10 minutes.
6. Top the steaks with a generous slice of the herb/garlic butter and serve along with oven baked potatoes. Consider offering potato toppings such as sour cream, green onion or chives, cheese, bacon bits etc.

Dessert:

So-Easy Chocolate Cream Pie

A smart man knows how to win the heart of his date when he presents her with a chocolate pie he makes himself. This dessert certainly won my heart!

Directions:

Purchase a pre-made crust from the baking aisle in the grocery store, such as a graham cracker or shortbread crust. In the same aisle, you'll find boxed pudding mix; you can choose either instant chocolate, or cooked chocolate. All you'll need to add is milk, and the instructions are right on the box. The cooked pudding requires a little extra work but it's worth it. Make this a day ahead so it can chill. Serve with a can of whipped cream – a treat which you can use later in the bedroom!

Couple Cuddle Time

End your delightful evening on the couch with your arm around your girl, watching one of these favorite romantic comedies:

9 to 5
Sleepless in Seattle
Annie Hall
Groundhog Day
Silver Linings Playbook
Four Weddings and a Funeral
Moonstruck
Splash
Waitress
Breakfast at Tiffany's
50 First Dates
Notting Hill
As Good as it Gets
Love Actually
Roxanne

Making Great Memories

When A Man Loves A Woman Toolbox

Many of the following items can be found at:
www.makinggreatmemories.com/shop/

The 5 Love Languages by Gary Chapman
Flowers
Single flower and a few wrapped chocolates for the bedroom
Candles or LED lights
Table cloth or placemats
Proper place settings, including all tableware, glasses, dishes etc.
Sexy apron
MadLibs

Notes & Memories

Notes & Memories

6

From Palette To Palate

Introduction

When I was single and living quite frugally, one of my favorite free activities was strolling through the city streets during the First Friday Art Walks downtown. Sipping complimentary wine and looking at beautiful artwork with my girlfriends were things I very much looked forward to each month. Creative expression has always inspired me, whether it's on canvas, down the runway, or on a plate. I love exploring how others express themselves creatively. In fact, I ended up meeting the love of my life over a piece of art. First introduced at a fundraiser, we found each other bidding on the same piece of artwork. He won the bid, but I won the guy! Indeed, we won each other! The piece we were both bidding on is the most precious artwork we own.

I believe there is an artist in each of us and maybe you haven't discovered this about yourself yet. To quote Pablo Picasso, "Every child is an artist, the problem is staying an artist when you grow up." Perhaps this theme night will inspire conversation about artistic opportunities. Talk about enrolling in a class. Local colleges and adult community centers offer several forms of artistic expression such as photography, painting, jewelry design, woodworking, stained glass, pottery, quilting, glassblowing, guitar, piano, acting, writing, cooking, cake decorating, interior design, gardening, etc.

Also consider planning a future date night at a Paint Night where you can socialize, drink wine and paint. These are very popular in most towns. It would be fun to get a caricature done by a local artist or commission an artist to paint a portrait of you and your significant other. Attend a gallery opening, stroll through an art museum, or go on an art walk where you can engage in conversation with the artists. The world is your canvas!

Starting With The Blank Canvas

If you have never thought of yourself as an artist, that is all about to change! Art is an expression of many forms, and you will be unleashing your inner artist with this theme through painting, culinary arts, musically, and theatrically . . . especially in the bedroom. The first stroke on your canvas is to set the tone for the week. If you'll be using the Love Is Art couples kit (link to purchase in Toolbox at end of this chapter), give a piece of the equipment to your loved one each day of the week leading up to your special evening. Again, Friday is an excellent choice for a theme night. You could start the week on Monday by giving him the slippers (from the Love is Art kit), followed by the body scrubber on Tuesday, then the painter's tarp, the canvas on Thursday, and finally, the paint on Friday, at your art opening. Your loved one will probably be confused by the pieces in your kit, but I promise they'll be thrilled when they find out what your plans are.

Getting Ready for the Art Opening

You may want to loosen up your partner with an artist inspired cocktail before you tell him what your plans are for the evening. The Bellini originated in 1948 by a bartender named Giuseppe Cipriani at Harry's Bar in Venice. The colors of the cocktail reminded him of the hues used by the famous Renaissance painter Giovanni Bellini. (Coincidentally, the same bartender created Carpaccio, a favorite appetizer of rare roast beef named after the painter Vittore Carpaccio who used vivid red colors in his work). Cipriani certainly understood the uplifting power of art! An alternative would be to serve Chardonnay wine in a plastic cup and cubed cheese, which is what hosts typically serve to guests at an art opening.

While sipping on your Bellinis and nibbling on Carpaccio, consider setting up your dining table or coffee table with a blank sheet of paper and scattering about markers or crayons - have fun drawing pictures or sending each other love notes. Get creative and remember, nobody is judging what you're doing.

Music

"Where words leave off, music begins" - Heinrich Heine

Music is another essential art form for this date night, to be enjoyed by listening and also through dance. My aesthetic preference for this theme is to play classical music by the composers Mozart, Beethoven and Bach, but you may be more inspired by other musical genres or to use the following song suggestions with an artist theme:

Don McLean, "Vincent"
Nat King Cole, "Mona Lisa"
Norah Jones, "Painter Song"
Rolling Stones, "Paint it Black"
Talking Heads, "Artists Only"
Rufus Wainwright, "Art Teacher"
Modern Lovers, "Pablo Picasso"
David Bowie, "Andy Warhol"

The Art Opening

When you feel the timing is right, give your partner the final gift from the Love Is Art kit - the body paint. Now you get to explain the special point of the evening: you and your partner are going to create an abstract painting, by getting naked, covering each other in body paint, and rolling around on the canvas. When dry, the canvas can be stretched, framed and hung in your home - maybe over your bed! The best part is that only you and your partner will know what it is, and you'll always have the memory of the passion you shared in creating it. If anything, you'll have a really good laugh!

Never Stop Creating

If covering yourself with paint and rolling on a canvas isn't your thing, then perhaps you would be interested in edible body paint. It's so much fun, and so delicious; you could do it as an alternative activity or even dessert. There are many websites to purchase body paints, or you can make it at home using vanilla pudding (I use the pre-made four packs because it looks like a paint palette) and add natural colors, like from beet juice or mashed avocado, to create your palette. If using food coloring, beware, it does stain the skin temporarily. Use the stroke of a brush to create your passionate designs or perhaps you're more into finger painting. You can also purchase glow-in-the dark body paint, or pens with edible ink, which are fun to use for drawing tattoos on one another. You could also use squeeze bottles filled with toppings during the dessert portion of the night, such as warm chocolate syrup or caramel. Be careful of the temperature and of anything that might get harder or stickier after exposure to air.

If you're doing either of these art forms, make sure you use the purchased, non-toxic kit, and follow the directions. Both activities could be quite messy and could stain surfaces.

Food as Art:

Isn't it a delightful experience to dine in a fine restaurant that presents you with a meal that looks like a work of art? As much as I am impressed with the presentation, I often leave those restaurants with an empty stomach and an empty wallet. This menu is a beautiful relationship between food and art, that isn't just fun and creative, it's delicious and satisfying! At the beginning of the week, I presented my partner with a menu that I had drawn free-hand and placed it in a picture frame complete with an easel. We enjoyed looking at it all week as we anticipated our date night.

The Art Opening

~~~

The Bellini
Carpaccio
Cubist Salad inspired by artist Pablo Picasso
The main course of Landscape and Seascape featuring:
Landscape of Beef Tenderloin and Seascape of Pan-Seared Scallops
Beach Rose Potatoes and Garden Vegetables
Artisan Bread, herb butter
LOVE Brownie Silhouettes inspired by artist Robert Indiana

Recipes:

The Bellini

Directions:

The Bellini is two parts prosecco to one part fresh peach puree (traditionally with white peaches, you can purchase peach nectar at most grocery stores) To make; chill a champagne flute, add the puree to the glass and pour in the sparkling wine, stir gently. Use sparkling juice or seltzer for a nonalcoholic version.

Carpaccio

Serves 2

Ingredients:

    A very small piece of fresh beef sirloin (3 oz)
    lemon
    olive oil
    kosher salt and fresh ground pepper
    Fresh parmesan cheese shavings
    micro-greens

Directions:

1. Place the sirloin in a freezer for 30 minutes or so, that way it's easier to shave thinly. Slice the rare beef as thin as possible and place it in a pretty design on your serving plate.
2. Drizzle with olive oil, salt and pepper and a squeeze of lemon.
3. Use the same ingredients in step 2 and mix with microgreens to mound on top of the beef.
4. Serve with parmesan shavings atop the microgreens and a lemon wedge.

Cubist Salad

You will truly feel like an artist when you prepare this most unusual salad in the shape of a Rubik's Cube.

Serves 2

Ingredients:
- avocado
- watermelon
- feta block
- micro-greens
- mint
- 1 T fresh lemon juice or white wine vinegar
- ¼ cup olive oil
- kosher salt and fresh ground black pepper

Directions:

1. Cut the avocado, watermelon and cheese equally into cubes ½ inch -1 inch in size.
2. Arrange them alternating into a 3x3 cube that resembles a Rubik's Cube.
3. In a small jar, shake the olive oil with the vinegar and salt and pepper. Place microgreens on top of cube, sprinkle with mint and drizzle with dressing.

Beach Rose Potatoes

These potatoes are as much fun to make as they are to eat and they really do look like beach roses!

Serves 2

Ingredients:

- 2 red potatoes (don't peel), sliced very thin, preferably with a mandoline
- salted water
- 2T melted butter
- kosher salt and fresh ground pepper
- 1 tsp fresh rosemary minced or ½ tsp dried rosemary
- 2 T grated Parmigiano-Reggiano cheese
- 1 egg beaten

Directions:

1. Grease 4 muffin tins with melted butter reserving the leftover butter for potatoes.
2. Bring salted water to a boil in a medium sized pot, then place potato slices in the water and cook for 3 minutes until pliable.
3. Drain and cool enough to handle, then toss with salt, pepper, rosemary and grated cheese.
4. Preheat oven 400 degrees F.
5. In a small dish, beat the egg, then add 2 tsp of egg to each muffin cup.
6. Start with the largest slices first and, from the outside in, overlap your potato slices in circles, finishing with the smallest slices in the middle. Half slices are good to use in the middle.
7. Spoon the remaining egg into the 4 cups and brush the potato roses with leftover butter.

8. Bake for 10 minutes at 400 degrees F, then reduce the temperature to 300 degrees F and continue to bake another 20 minutes.
9. Slide a sharp knife around the potatoes and take out of pan when ready to serve. Potato roses can be prepared ahead of time and reheated.

Pan-Seared Scallops

Scallops are my most favorite seafood, and this is my favorite way to prepare them. Here they are used as a smaller portion to be accompanied with beef tenderloin for the sea and landscape menu, but you can certainly use them as a "stand alone" dish. To purchase the most delicious Maine scallops, go to www.Downeastdayboat.com.

Serves 2

Ingredients:
- ½ pound of scallops, preferably fresh and large
- ¼ cup Italian bread crumbs
- 1 T unsalted butter
- 1 T olive oil
- ½ fresh lemon
- freshly grated parmesan cheese

Directions:

1. Rinse scallops, remove the muscle, and dry with paper towel.
2. Roll in Italian bread crumbs.
3. Heat a nonstick skillet over med high heat. Add olive oil and butter. When butter melts, add scallops flat side down and not touching. Cook about 2 minutes, flip the scallops, then remove skillet from heat. Cover with grated parmesan cheese, juice squeezed from half a lemon and place a cover over the pan. Assemble your serving plate with the beach rose potatoes, vegetables and beef, then add your scallops. A work of art!

LOVE Brownie Silhouette with Fruit Drizzle

This is a simple dessert made with a box of your favorite brownie mix.

Ingredients:

1 package brownie mix (avoid mixes with nuts, chips etc, they interfere with the sculpture)

Fruit topping used for ice cream, such as raspberry or strawberry, warmed up in a squeeze bottle.

Favorite ice cream or whipped cream or both

Mint for garnish

Directions:

1. Make brownies according to directions. Cool completely.
2. Carefully cut brownies into the letters L-O-V-E and place them on a pretty serving platter to create the iconic design from the artist Robert Indiana.
3. When ready to serve, place a letter on a serving plate and create designs around the letter using the fruit topping from a squeeze bottle.
4. Add ice cream, whipped cream and a sprig of mint.

The Art of Presentation:

A Quick Lesson on Nutrition, Garnishing and Platescaping:

Plating is the art of presenting food by making it visual and stimulating to the senses. Consider these tips:

1. Nutrition: A nutritiously balanced plate isn't just crucial for optimum health throughout your life, but the visual appeal with all it's color and texture will make you want to eat it! All your meals should include 50% Vegetables, 25% Protein and 25% starch. Mix in some fruit and dairy throughout the day. www.Choosemyplate.gov is a very informational website on nutrition.

2. Taste and Texture: Flavors need to compliment each other. Spicy with cool. Soft, rich foods plate well with something crunchy.

3. Visual Appeal: If it looks good, we want to eat it! It's all about color. Dark rich color tends to have more nutrients. Picture this: A plate with a plain chicken breast, mashed potatoes and corn = boring! And, not the most diverse nutrients. Now visualize this: A plate with a chicken breast covered with tomato, mozzarella, and basil, oven roasted red potatoes (keep the skins on), carrots and broccoli = I want to eat that! When you plate the food, set it on the plate like a clock. Starch at 11 o'clock, vegetables at 2 o'clock and protein at 6 o'clock.

Think of your plate like a painting. Food is the medium and the rim of the plate is the frame. You are the artist and your plating style is uniquely your own. Go a little crazy and use these tips to help you create, create, create.

- Use white plates; they are the perfect canvas. Try square and oval for something different.

- Use a garnish that relates to the dish. For example, lemon often pairs with seafood. Scallions are nice if onions are in the dish. Make 1 inch slices on each end and place them in ice water, they curl up for a fun garnish.

- Herbs add color. A sprinkle of parsley or paprika adds visual interest. Toss micro- greens mixed with a little olive oil on side plates or atop meat or soup.

- Grow a herb garden outside your kitchen door or on a window sill. If possible, always use fresh herbs in recipes, and as a garnish. Keep a bouquet of herbs on your kitchen counter. Many grocery stores sell window sill pots of mixed herbs.

- Play with the height of food on a plate. Stacking food can be fun.

- Use the Rule of Odds. Plate food in quantities of three, five, or seven. This rule might apply to something like scallops or asparagus spears.

- Serve warm food on a pre-warmed plate and cold foods on a chilled plate.

- Purchase a few squeeze bottles to create plate designs for dinner and dessert sauces. Impress your guests by learning a few design strokes with your squeeze bottle. There is nothing quite like a chocolate spiderweb or a spoon drag. Make it simple by purchasing ice cream toppings, such as strawberry and chocolate, even condensed milk can be used to achieve greatness in your artwork.

- A microplane, zester or carrot peeler are essential tools for creating that extra special touch. Zest citrus fruits, microplane your parmesan cheese and make chocolate curls with a peeler. The texture adds so much depth and appeal to your plate, and even to our taste buds.

Inspiration for Cuddle Time:

Watch any movie with an artist theme such as:

Girl with a Pearl Earring
Frida
Mr Turner
Edvard Munch
My Left Foot
Big Eyes

Making Great Memories

Palette to Palate Toolbox

Many of the following items can be found at:
www.makinggreatmemories.com/shop/

Love Is Art Couples Kit
markers, crayons and butcher paper
body paints
squeeze bottles
Palette to Palate photos at www.makinggreatmemories.com/gallery

Notes & Memories

Notes & Memories

7

Anniversary Quickie

Introduction:

I know some years we just don't have the time or money to plan an amazing anniversary celebration, but I believe our wedding or dating anniversaries always deserve our attention. Nothing says, "I love you" more than investing time in each other. So if there's ever an opportunity to create a memory, do it! You can't afford not to celebrate, and that's why I created this "quickie" that can be put together in a few hours.

When you call or text during the workday to wish your lover a happy anniversary, tell them that you have a special evening planned. If they offer to help, suggest they bring home takeout for dinner - perhaps takeout from the restaurant where you had your first date. If you're planning a happy hour with appetizers, suggest something light for the main meal.

Atmosphere:

Create your environment and consider using a different place in the house or someplace that is significant to your relationship. I planned our little rendezvous in our downstairs family room where we keep the couch we were on when we had our first kiss. You could also tailgate someplace with a view, have a picnic at the beach, the park, etc.

Decorate a table with a little bouquet of seasonal flowers or plants. I used daisies and pussy willows because it was spring. Add a candle, special wine that you've shared before, and music that's significant to your relationship. Maybe music from your first concert or the background tunes that were playing when you shared your first kisses. Everyone has a relationship song or artist, and if you don't have one, now is the time to establish it together! A "together" song could be an excellent gift for you and your partner - if you share with him some personal lyrics or even try to decide on a song together by sharing what you value most about your connection.

What to Wear?

Time to prettify. I suggest wearing something you know your partner likes. If there's an outfit, he's bought you, wear that, or a dress you know he loves. I remember the outfit I was wearing when my husband and I met; perhaps that's an option for you too. I also like having a reason to shop, so I bought myself a pair of seriously blinged-out jeans and a simple white shirt that immediately caught his attention the moment he walked through the door. Complete the outfit with jewelry he's given you and the perfume he likes.

Happy Hour

A good choice for the happy hour is a substantial cheese board to accompany the drinks. An anniversary is a very special night, so now's the time to indulge in high-quality cheese – especially because you'll be saving on the takeout for dinner. First, find a cheesemonger in your town. Most towns have a gourmet cheese store, and some grocery stores have experts within the store to assist you. Bring along a cheeseboard, and many of these establishments will put it all together beautifully for you at no extra charge. I always have a great experience when I shop specialty stores, and it's fun to consult with people who know their stuff! With help, I created a charcuterie and cheese board that included smoked meats paired with a variety of cheeses from around the world. I cut the paper tags off the cheese wrappers and with toothpicks I made them into little flags to stick into the cheese...a United Nations of Cheese! You can add a variety of olives, smoked almonds, a ripe pear and a cluster of little champagne grapes. Don't forget the recommended crackers. This platter becomes a beautiful work of art without much effort. As a gift suggestion, consider joining a monthly cheese club to an online store such as Murray's Cheese.

The Cocktail

Consider creating a cocktail that's significant to the two of you. Perhaps a cocktail with the name The French Kiss, Sex Appeal, The Wedding Anniversary or Sex on the Beach. You could also peruse the wine aisle and search for "theme" wine based on the label such as Handsome Devil or Love Noir Pinot Noir. My partner and I came together after each experiencing the difficulty of divorce. After all the lessons we learned during that time, we now take a positive approach, with the motto: "When life gives you lemons, make lemonade." Our signature cocktail is the Lemon Drop! Here's my favorite recipe:

Lemon Drop Martini

Serves 1

Ingredients:
- 1 ½ oz vodka
- ½ oz orange liquor (optional)
- ½ oz simple syrup (more or less depending on your sweetness meter)
- 1 oz freshly squeezed lemon juice
- ice cubes
- superfine sugar for the rims
- lemon twist

Directions:
To make simple syrup: bring ½ cup sugar and ½ cup water to a boil in a medium saucepan. Boil 5 min without stirring. Let cool completely. Store in refrigerator.

To make cocktail: Put the martini glass in the freezer to chill while making the drink. Mix vodka, orange liqueur, simple syrup and lemon juice in a shaker. Fill with ice and shake vigorously. Strain and pour into the martini glass that has a sugar rim and lemon twist. Sugar rim is made by taking a lemon wedge and running it along the side of the glass and then dipping the glass into the superfine sugar. Grating lemon or orange zest into the sugar is a fun and tasty addition.

Together Time

Consider this idea while enjoying your charcuterie board and sipping on cocktails. I love that our phones have incredible cameras and I am in the habit of taking pictures incessantly. I don't know if it's my age or what, but I can't remember a lot of things! Capturing a moment with a few photos helps. Download your pictures onto a bigger screen such as a laptop, iPad or even a TV. Take the pictures from the past year, put them to music in a slideshow and create a little journey down memory lane. It's a great way to reflect, reminisce and relive the wonderful memories the two of you share, and it's incredibly easy! It is my tradition to create this slideshow every year, and my husband always looks forward to it. I have also created thoughtful books and fun calendars with these pictures. The first Christmas we shared together, it touched my husband's heart when I surprised him with a very thoughtful book all about our first year together, and he surprised me when he reacted with tears. Nothing will warm your heart more than to give a man the opportunity to express his sensitive side. When a man allows himself to be that vulnerable, you will know he's falling in love. Taking the time to create that book was my way of letting him know how much I appreciate our time together. Everyone needs to feel appreciation and giving your time to a loved one is what this book is all about. There are several places where you can easily make photo books, such as Shutterfly, Snapfish, and Walmart.

The Happy Ending

What is your partner's favorite dessert? Perhaps you could make it for him. Early in our relationship, I asked my partner about his most favorite homemade dessert from childhood. I remembered his original answer—red velvet cake—and so for our anniversary, I baked him a red velvet cake in the shape of a heart. That simple gesture became a very thoughtful memory. I've included the recipe, but if you are in a time crunch, you could use a pre-made cake mix and cut the cake into a heart shape after it's done baking. And finally, as an easy dessert, find a cupcake bakery in your hometown. They are as much fun as the cheese store, and it's great to support local business.

Red Velvet Heart Cake

Ingredients for cake:
- 2 1/2 cups all purpose flour
- 1 tsp salt
- 2 cups of sugar
- 1 cup butter, softened
- 2 eggs
- 2 T cocoa powder
- 3 T liquid red food coloring
- 1 cup buttermilk
- 1 tsp vanilla extract
- 1 1/2 tsp baking soda
- 1 T distilled white vinegar or cider vinegar

Directions:

1. Preheat oven to 350 degrees F.
2. Grease and lightly flour 2 round 9" cake pans.
3. In a medium bowl, sift flour and salt together, set aside.
4. In a large bowl, mix the butter and sugar until light and fluffy. Add the eggs one at a time, beating well.
5. Next, add the flour mixture to the bowl alternately with the buttermilk and vanilla.
6. In a small custard dish, mix the red food coloring and cocoa powder until a paste forms. Add to the cake mixture. Continue to mix well.
7. In another custard dish, stir together the baking soda and vinegar. Gently fold the foamy mixture into the batter. Do not mix or beat the batter after this is added.
8. Scrape batter evenly into pans - batter will be very thick. Make sure batter is level.
9. Bake for 25-30 minutes, or until cake springs back when pressed in the center. Turn out on cooling racks and cool completely.

Cream Cheese Frosting

Ingredients:
- 2 - 8oz packages of cream cheese, softened
- 1 cup butter, softened
- 2 tsp vanilla extract
- 4-5 cups sifted confectioners' sugar

Directions:

1. In a large mixing bowl, beat the cream cheese, butter and vanilla together until smooth.
2. With the mixer on low, gradually add the confectioners' sugar. Increase the speed to high and beat until light and fluffy. If mixture is too thick, add a little milk or cream. If it is too thin, add more confectioner's sugar.

Assembly:

If making cake into a heart shape, create a template with a piece of waxed paper in the shape of a heart. With a serrated knife, cut both cakes into a heart shape. Frost the bottom layer, then add the top layer and finish with remaining frosting on sides and top. You could also take the remaining cake chunks and crumble them into fine pieces and sprinkle all over the cake while the frosting is sticky.

Cuddle Time:

Here's a list of romantic movies to end your anniversary theme night:

Princess Bride
Ever After
A Walk to Remember
The Vow
Time Traveler's Wife
While You Were Sleeping
Love Story
Somewhere in Time
The Proposal
My Big Fat Greek Wedding

Making Great Memories

Anniversary Quickie Toolbox

Cheesemonger
Cheeseboard or pretty platter
A year in pictures
Special cocktail/wine
Special dessert

Notes & Memories

8

Japaneasy

Introduction:

Culture has always intrigued me. Growing up in a small town, in a little corner of the United States, I wasn't exposed to many cultures. I'd never eaten Chinese food until I went to college and "sushi" wasn't a word I had ever heard. My roommate was Lebanese, and my first teaching job was among a community of Greeks who exposed me to wonderful family recipes and heritage. It wasn't until those early adult years that I discovered my love of good food and so I enjoyed the company of others who had a passion for it. To quote Julia Child, "People who love to eat are always the best people." That led me to many years working in restaurants and using the extra cash for dining out. Even though I've never had formal culinary training, I do have an adventurous palate when it comes to food. I like to eat where the locals eat, I like ethnic food, and I like to learn new cooking skills. It was a happy day when restaurants started "open kitchens" so you can watch the chef. Nothing has intrigued me more than opportunities to sit at a chef's table or watch my meal during preparation. Japaneasy is a theme reflecting that joy. It's fascinating to go to a Japanese steakhouse to watch a Hibachi chef demonstrate his knife skills or sit at a sushi bar and witness the creation of fresh sushi rolls. Inspiring, to say the least!

This theme can be put together rather quickly depending on the amount of time and effort you want to dedicate to it. Although it's considered a "quickie," it could also be used for a birthday or anniversary celebration. After all, any man would enjoy coming home to a Geisha girl! To keep it simple, pick up sushi at your local grocery store or Japanese take-out. I also love to make my own sushi rolls and so have included the recipe. Sushi rolls are fun to assemble and much easier than you may realize. I learned watching YouTube and, though most sushi chefs would roll their eyes at me, I find immense gratification in doing it myself. My end of the week bento boxes are made by simply cleaning out my refrigerator of leftovers and serving it up in a creative way.

The Teaser:

Inform your partner that he will be coming home to a Geisha girl. A Geisha girl is a Japanese female entertainer who acts as a hostess and whose skills include performing various Japanese arts such as classical music, dance, games, and conversation. To become a Geisha girl is an honorable and discreet process. Most readers would not qualify for this title, but you can watch videos of Geisha girls dancing and perhaps attempt that artistic form . . . or at least get a paper fan and flirt.

Zen-like Atmosphere:

For this theme, I am going to suggest creating your evening in two places around your home. The living room and the bedroom. To create the proper Japanese-inspired atmosphere, you should include these five elements: fire (candles), water (fountain, vase with flowers), earth (earth colors, stones), wood (bamboo placemat, plants) and metal (brass candle stick or bowl).

The living room decor starts by focusing on the coffee table with a scatter of floor cushions surrounding it. To create a Zen-like atmosphere, declutter around the table and decorate with earth colors of tan, brown, grey or green. Consider earth tone placemats like bamboo, wood or fabric made of linen in muted colors (no prints). Add candles made from natural elements of soy or beeswax placed in a clean votive glass. A bonsai plant or cherry blossom branch would be a nice touch. It would also be fun to include a tabletop Zen garden with a little rake to make the sand designs helpful for meditation purposes. Fire-up the tabletop fountain if you have one. Fold cloth napkins into a lotus flower and put out the chopsticks. (Video instructions can be found at www.makinggreatmemories.com). Add sake cups if you so desire and a traditional Japanese teapot with cups.

In the bedroom, to create a sanctuary that is zen-like, you must begin with a clean and decluttered room. Think minimalist. Create soft lighting by placing votive candles around the room and maybe cherry blossom branches on the nightstands. Place a tray on the bed to be used for your sushi and martinis. Have your music ready.

Music:

Traditional Japanese music can be found using your computer or other personal devices and streaming through YouTube, iTunes, Pandora, Google music, etc. Look for titles like "Japanese Zen" with traditional flute, koto, and shamisen.

Gift suggestion:

Many people enjoy Japanese Anime, so if this is something your partner likes, consider commissioning an artist to draw the both of you as Anime Avatars. You can find many talented artists who offer this service at websites like Etsy and Fiverr. If you grew up playing with Pokemon cards, gather a deck or consider downloading the app Pokemon Go.

Geisha Girl:

You can get as traditional as you want for the look of a Geisha Girl by exploring many "how to" websites. I put my hair up in a big, soft bun and added a few chopsticks even though I know it's not traditional. You could also put a pretty flower or fan in your hair. Paint your lips bright red and pencil your eyes into almond shapes. Wear a kimono if you have one. I found a beautiful Japanese kimono at a consignment shop. You could also wear a silky negligee, but if you really want to please your gentleman, go to my website www.makinggreatmemories.com/shop/ to check out the sexy Geisha girl costume and how you can purchase it. One final accessory… Create a temporary tattoo using a black eye pencil or edible ink and write, "I love you" in Japanese on the inside of your thigh! You can find that image with an internet search.

Time to get your Zen on!

Timing is everything with this night. Coordinate your evening to begin the moment your partner walks through the door. One of the most memorable scenes from *Sex in the City* was Samantha Jones naked on the table, covered in sushi. If that seems a little over the top, then have the sushi ready on the bedroom tray along with the martinis. Candles lit, music playing and you, the Geisha girl, glowing on the bed.

Food

The Menu

Green Tea Martini or Warm Sake
Homemade Vegetable Sushi Rolls
Clean-Out-The-Refrigerator Bento Box
Traditional Japanese Dessert

Cocktail

Green Tea and Ginger Martini

Serves 1

Ingredients:

    2 oz lemon vodka

    1 oz green tea iced tea with ginseng and honey

    1 oz ginger simple syrup (water, sugar, fresh ginger: directions below)

    1 lemon slice

    1 piece crystallized ginger

Directions:

1. To make simple ginger syrup, combine in a small saucepan ½ cup water, ½ cup sugar + 2 T grated fresh ginger and bring to boil over medium-high heat for 5 minutes. Remove and cool.
2. To make the cocktail, place in a shaker the lemon vodka, green iced tea, simple syrup and fill with ice. Shake vigorously for 30 seconds. Strain the drink into a martini glass. Garnish with lemon slice and crystallized ginger.

To make without alcohol, just omit the lemon vodka and increase the iced tea.

Appetizer:

Homemade Vegetable Sushi Rolls

I suggest searching for videos on how to make sushi on the internet or visit my YouTube Channel at http://www.makinggreatmemories.com/videos to watch my simpler, homemade version.
Makes 3 Sushi Rolls

Ingredients:

    1 cup sushi rice (makes 3 cups cooked rice)
    1 ¼ cup water
    2T mirin (sweet rice wine)
    3 sheets nori
    Use any vegetables you like. The following vegetables should be cut julienne (very thin strips): carrots, red pepper, yellow pepper, green onion, cucumber seeded. Also consider; avocado and pickled ginger.
    toasted Sesame seeds or black sesame seeds
    sushi dipping sauce (recipe follows)

Directions for Rice:

Make rice according to directions on package. When done, sprinkle with 2T mirin and keep in a wooden bowl covered with a towel.

Directions for Sushi:

1. Place a bamboo sushi roller flat on the counter with the bamboo reeds horizontal to you. You can usually find sushi rollers in most grocery stores and Asian markets.
2. Place nori sheet on top and moisten lightly with mirin. With wet hands, press 1 cup rice on top of nori, leaving 1 ½ inch edges on the top and bottom, but pressing it all to the sides. Press evenly and smooth.

3. Start building your vegetables in a horizontal stripe, making them tight and straight. Place a layer of pickled ginger on top.
4. To roll the sushi, pick up the farthest edge of the bamboo roller and hold it with the nori, then pull it up over the vegetable strips and press the roller. Keep rolling and pressing to make a round tube. Repeat with the two remaining nori.
5. Wrap sushi rolls in plastic wrap and store refrigerated until ready.
6. To serve, slice off the ends with a very sharp knife and slice each roll into 8 pieces. Sprinkle with sesame seeds. Serve on a platter with pickled ginger and Sushi Dipping Sauce. Don't forget the chopsticks!

Sushi Dipping Sauce

Ingredients:
- ¼ tsp red pepper flakes
- ½ tsp pickled ginger or fresh ginger, minced
- 1 tsp minced green onion
- 2 T white wine vinegar
- 2 T soy sauce
- 1/2 tsp sesame oil

Directions:

Combine all ingredients in a small bowl and serve as a dipping sauce for the sushi.

Main Course:

Clean-Out-The-Refrigerator Bento Boxes With Warm Sake

Directions:

    If you don't have traditional Bento boxes, use a wooden box or tray. I found Asian-inspired wooden boxes at the Dollar Store. Place your dinner ingredients into large paper muffin cups in your Bento box. Be creative and use leftovers from the past week. My Bento box included: Asian slaw mix, small wraps, pineapple slices, carrot coins, potato chips, pickles and traditional Japanese tea cookies. Serve with chopsticks in your zen-like living room.

Dessert:

Mochi found at an Asian market
Green tea cookies from Japan
Green tea ice cream (matcha) found in some grocery stores

Cuddle Time:

Relax for the rest of the evening, watching one of these Japanese/American films:

Memoirs of a Geisha
Lost in Translation
The Last Samurai
Wolverine
Sayonara
Shogun

Making Great Memories

Japaneasy Toolbox

Many of the following items can be found at:
www.makinggreatmemories.com/shop/

2 Bento boxes or sturdy wooden boxes or baskets
Asian-inspired placemats (wooden, linen, bamboo)
Soy candles
Cherry blossom, exotic flower, Ikebana
Zen table top garden
2 large cloth napkins
Sake cups, tea cups, Japanese tea pot
Kimono, Geisha girl costume or silky negligee
Sushi tray
Sushi mat
Chopsticks
JapanEasy video @ http://www.makinggreatmemories.com/videos

Notes & Memories

Notes & Memories

9

Role Play Getaway: Cowboy Up!

Hey, y'all!

As a schoolteacher, I never had much money to buy expensive gifts, but was blessed with the gift of creativity which I used in both my career and personal life. I wanted to do something unusual and memorable for the sweet man in my life but wasn't able to go crazy buying him pricey items. Instead, I came up with a fun, imaginative experience for us to share, which is really what this book is all about! I decided to create a western cowboy theme for his birthday. I found a historical, boutique hotel and thought it would be a hoot to stay there for a night. Coincidentally, the hotel was next to a BBQ joint, which fit perfectly into the western theme. That's what gets my heart pumping—when things just fall into place. I have as much fun planning it all as I do during the experience. While I realize that things don't always fall that perfectly into place, you could create this evening in any hotel, and BBQ joints aren't usually hard to find. I've also included a cowboy-inspired menu, in case you prefer to spend this evening home-on-the-range.

Howdy, Partner!

Before leaving the house with my saddlebag of tricks, I left my sweetie a Tellagami message (a modern-day telegraph). For those of you who have never used it, www.Tellagami.com allows you to create an animated character with an app on your phone, tablet or other device. The fun thing about Tellagami is that you can make the character look like you and talk like you. It's a much more playful way to send a message, especially if the message is a special evening together! Once I left the house, my Tellagami instructed my birthday boy to go upstairs in our home, where he was to find the next clue to his birthday celebration. On the bed were his cowboy boots and his western hat. The next message sent him to the boutique hotel, where another message was waiting with the desk clerk. The final message directed him to our hotel room.

*The moment I opened the door for my cowboy, was the moment he has never *forgotten and the reason this theme is my husband's favorite. He still talks about it four years later!*

Fixin' to Fandango:

I wanted to create a western theme that brought us back into the time of saloons and brothels. I replaced the bulbs in the bed lamps with red bulbs and set my battery-operated candles around the room. Make sure you remember a deck of cards (preferably the traditional Hoyle cards established in 1672), checkers or backgammon, and a few poker chips. Complete the hoedown between the sheets with music from your portable speakers using the suggested genres.

An All-American Jamboree:

Country music, Folk, Americana, Bluegrass.

No Calico for this Cow-Bunny:

As stated before, put your guy in a cowboy hat, boots and a nice pair of Levi's. (all-American and oh-so-sexy!) When he knocks on the door, greet him as a very memorable cowgirl. Maybe your look includes a cute brassiere with cut-off jeans and a girlish ponytail or braids. Most important are the cowgirl boots. Listen, girls, if you don't own a pair of cowgirl boots, then board the next plane to Texas and get a pair! They are incredibly comfortable and will make you look fabulous. I've never worn anything that has given me as many compliments as my red cowgirl boots. To me, red is the only choice, but choose whatever color makes you feel sexy.

If you want to give your cowboy a distinct memory, I suggest you greet him as a saloon girl. You can achieve this look by wearing a corset and a pair of silk or net stockings held up with a garter belt. If you are interested in this look, visit my website, www.makinggreatmemories.com/shop/ for links and information. Finally, don't forget the attitude - saloon girls didn't put up with any disrespectful cowboys and usually packed a pistol in their boots. (I'm certainly not suggesting you do that though!)

Shuck Those Clothes and Call My Bluff!

Bring out the playing cards and the poker chips for a game of couple's strip poker. Or go to a country western joint and do a little line dancing. Is there a rodeo in town or a place to ride an electronic bull? Go horseback riding. Cuddle up around a backyard campfire under the stars complete with cowboy coffee served in tin cups.

The Whole Kit and Caboodle:

A few gift suggestions to consider would be a Stetson hat or boots, but that can be difficult to purchase unless you know the exact size. Less expensive gift ideas for your cowboy might be an authentic leather belt or Stetson cologne. Surprise him with a trip to a dude ranch in Arizona, Colorado or Wyoming. Visit Oklahoma City, home of the National Cowboy and Western Heritage Museum.

Wet Yer Whistle:

A bottle of Jack Daniels with a few rocks glasses would probably work best for this cowboy theme or a microbrew beer that has some western theme. Payette Brewing company has labels like Rustler, Mutton Buster, and Rodeo. I've also included a recipe for a Prickly Pear Margarita, which I thought matched nicely with the red boots. For a mocktail, offer something like sarsaparilla.

Prickly Pear Cactus Margarita

This margarita is a concoction made with prickly pear syrup, which may be difficult to find in some locations. If you live in the Southwest, you could make your own syrup. Be careful of the thorns though!

Serves 1

Ingredients:
- coarse salt, as needed
- 2 oz tequila
- 2 oz sweet and sour mix
- 1 oz triple sec
- 1 oz lime juice
- 1 oz prickly pear syrup

Directions

1. Pour salt into a small plate. Wet the rim of a margarita glass and dip rim into salt.
2. Fill a cocktail shaker with ice; pour tequila, sweet and sour mix, triple sec, lime juice, and pear syrup over ice. Cover and shake drink; strain into prepared margarita glass garnished with a slice of lime.
3. This recipe can be made ahead of time and kept in a thermos for travel. Add the ice and shake upon serving.

Hankering for Vittles:

While bellied-up with a cocktail, your cowboy may be hankering for a few snacks. If you are in a hotel room, this may limit your options. I suggest a quick and easy snack of Cowboy Caviar and Cowboy Bark. Trader Joe's brand has perfect cowboy labels. TexMex 7 Layer Dip and beef jerky would also work well.

Come and Get it!

The dinner bell is ringing! If you're going out to a Texas Roadhouse, Dave's Famous BBQ or a local barbecue joint, I hope your vittles are tasty. If staying home-on-the-range is your thing, consider this chuckwagon menu. If interested in taking it up a notch, wrangle yourself a Pioneer Woman cookbook, sure to satisfy your cowboy's tastebuds.

Western Theme Menu

Prickly Pear Cactus Margarita
Cowboy Beans
Chipotle Slaw
Cheesy Jalapeno Cornbread
Texas Sheet Cake

Recipes

Easy Cowboy Beans

Servings: 6

Ingredients:
- ½ lb lean hamburger
- ½ cup chopped onion
- 6 slices pre-cooked bacon crumbled
- 2 16 oz can pork and beans (undrained)
- 2 16 oz can kidney beans (undrained)
- ¼ cup ketchup
- ¼ cup bbq sauce
- ¼ cup brown sugar
- 1 T prepared mustard
- 1 tsp chili powder

Directions:

1. In a frying pan, brown the hamburger and the onions.
2. Add the cooked meat to a crockpot or dutch oven. Then add all of the remaining ingredients, mixing to combine.
3. For crockpot, cover and cook on high for 2 hours or low for 4 hours. If cooking in dutch oven, butter the sides of your dish and cook uncovered at 350 degrees F for 1½ to 2 hrs.

Chipotle Slaw

Serves: 6

Ingredients:

    1/4 cup mayonnaise
    ¼ cup sour cream or plain Greek yogurt
    1 T sugar
    1 tsp lime zest
    1 T lime juice
    1 T white wine vinegar
    ½ tsp kosher salt
    ¼ tsp fresh ground pepper
    1 chipotle chili peppers in adobo sauce (canned). Remove seeds and finely chop.
    1 tsp adobo sauce from the can
    1 (16 oz) package of shredded coleslaw mix
    ½ cup cilantro chopped (optional)

Directions:

1. Mix all ingredients except the coleslaw mix and cilantro and pour into a serving bowl.
2. Add coleslaw and cilantro. Mix well to combine. Chill for at least 30 minutes.

Easy Cheesy Jalapeno Cornbread

Serves: 4

Ingredients:
- 1 (8.5 oz) box Jiffy cornbread mix
- 1 egg
- ⅓ cup milk
- 2 T canned jalapeno peppers diced or 1/2 T fresh jalapeno, minced
- 1 cup shredded cheddar cheese

Directions:

1. Combine all ingredients in a medium bowl. Mixture will be thick.
2. Grease 8 inch cast iron skillet, muffin tin or 8 inch baking pan.
3. Bake muffins 15-20 minutes or 8 inch skillet 20-25 minutes.

Texas Sheet Cake

This cake is huge! It's baked in the size of Texas, but is so delicious it will shrink to the size of Rhode Island in no time!
Serves: 12

Ingredients for cake:
- 1 cup butter melted
- 1 cup water
- ¼ cup cocoa powder
- 2 cups granulated sugar
- 2 cups flour
- ½ tsp kosher salt
- 1 tsp baking soda
- 2 eggs
- ½ cup sour cream or buttermilk
- 1 tsp vanilla

Directions:

1. Preheat oven 350 degrees F.
2. Spray an 11x16x1.5 inch jelly roll pan with nonstick spray.
3. In a large sauce pan on med-high heat, bring the butter, water and cocoa to a boil.
4. Remove from heat and add the rest of the ingredients. Mix with an electric mixer until smooth. Spread evenly in prepared 11x16 jelly roll pan and place in preheated oven.
5. Bake for 20 minutes. While sheet cake is baking, make the frosting, which goes on the cake as soon as it comes out of the oven.

Frosting

Ingredients:
- ½ cup butter
- ¼ cup cocoa
- ⅓ cup milk
- 1 lb box of confectioner's sugar
- 1 cup walnuts or pecans, chopped and toasted
- 1 tsp vanilla

Directions:

1. Bring butter, cocoa and milk to a boil on med-high heat.
2. Remove from heat and stir in the confectioner's sugar and nuts
3. Add the vanilla, stir well, and pour evenly over sheet cake as soon as it comes out of the oven.

Snuggle Time

Lasso your cowboy and snuggle up to one of these Western inspired movies:

Urban Cowboy
Blazing Saddles
The Magnificent Seven
Midnight Cowboy
Unforgiven
Butch Cassidy and the Sundance Kid
True Grit
City Slickers
Netflix series *Longmire*
Bonanza

Making Great Memories

Western Theme Toolbox

Many of the following items can be found at:
www.makinggreatmemories.com/shop/

Tellagami app or Western-themed cards to instruct your cowboy
Western Attire for Cowboys: Hat and boots. (You certainly don't have to be authentic. Be silly and get a child's hat, sheriff badge and handcuffs all from The Dollar Store.)
Sexy Western wear for cowgirls
Red light bulbs and LED lights
Hoyle playing cards, checkers or backgammon, poker chips
Cowboy-themed snacks, food and drinks using cowboy labels
Tableware, such as tin or enamelware
Red and white checkered napkins and tablecloth for that country look

Notes & Memories

10

Role Play Getaway: Italian Style

Introduction:

Sometimes it's fun pretending to be someone else. So when my partner and I won, at a silent auction, a night at a local, airport hotel and dinner at a nearby Italian restaurant, I thought it would be a bit crazy, and fun, to role-play our night. Luckily, I have a partner who goes along with my silly antics. While drinking our Saturday morning coffee in bed, we planned the whole event for that evening. The Italian restaurant triggered the idea of pretending to be Italians, but you could create any theme you like from a different restaurant or other inspiration. Imagine – who have you always imagined being for a day? Passionate Italian lovers? Smoldering Latin dancers? Playful French paramours? Get creative and drop any insecurities you might have – I promise, with a playful partner, this idea can be very silly and help build intimacy. If your partner is less excited, try letting him pick the theme – he might feel more comfortable, and even surprise you with his desires and creativity!

My honey and I modeled ourselves after a combination of characters from Jersey Shore and My Cousin Vinnie. I was to become Mona Lisa, and my partner was Vinnie. We're stuck in Portland, Maine because of a flight delay and we were not happy about it. We were big on accents and even bigger on attitude. I spent the day working out my look and wardrobe and gathering up all the hotel room essentials to make the evening memorable.

Once we got to the hotel, I was going to quickly change into my Mona Lisa outfit, adopt the role, and meet my Vinnie down at the bar in the hotel lobby. I intended to impress him with a hot Mediterranean look, and to throw in an attitude and accent while I sipped a Long Island Iced Tea. I had this plan working in my head all afternoon, but the moment the elevator door opened up in the lobby, everything changed. I suddenly heard a bunch of girls scream my name. Coming out of the elevator was a group of my eighth-grade students who were at the hotel for a pool party. Thank goodness I wasn't wearing the Mona Lisa look yet!

Plan B went into action very quickly. I didn't meet Vinnie at the bar. Instead, we had a little pre-dinner warm-up in our hotel room. As we were leaving the hotel to go to our Italian restaurant, I ran into those girls again on the elevator. What are the chances? This kind of thing tends to happen frequently in my life, so I've learned to just laugh at the circumstances. Thankfully in Maine, you dress in lots of winter layers and so although I had big Jersey hair, I don't think my Mona Lisa look was too revealing. I include this story here only to say that you never know what can happen – and a playful, spontaneous attitude will help overcome any surprises! Just roll with it, and fun will surely follow!

Dress Up

Dressing as an Italian Stallion is a relatively easy concept for the guys. I requested Vinnie wear the tightest jeans he had, paired with a button-down oxford and a gold chain. I also asked that he unbutton his shirt as low as he was willing to go, that he slicked his hair back, and tie everything together with a sleek pair of dress shoes. To become Mona Lisa, I sported a tight dress and wore my hair New Jersey style – teased and big! I had purchased hair extensions several years ago that are surprisingly easy to put in and which instantly make me feel super feminine. I used dark eye shadow and liner to create a dark, smoky look and added red lipstick and nails. High-heeled boots, big hoop earrings and a gold chain with an "M" on it completed my look. (The "M" was for my grandmother Mabelle, whose jewelry I still wear.) Don't forget to chew gum in an obnoxious way. Finally, the only things left to add are the accent and attitude.

Room for Passion

Place LED candles around the hotel room. Don't forget the little speakers to play your music. (I selected a Pandora playlist with my favorite Jersey boys, Bruce Springsteen and Bon Jovi.) Set out a small tray of cheese, crostini, red grapes and an aperitivo. This pre-dinner drink could be a glass of Chianti or Prosecco. You can also include a bottle of Pellegrino sparkling water. I have old silver wine glasses that are great for traveling because they're nearly unbreakable. After a few sips of the wine, Vinnie and Mona were very relaxed and happy to be stuck in this corner of the United States.

Dinner at the Trattoria

If you're pretending to be Italian, the drive to the restaurant can be quite amusing. Vinnie and I yelled, interrupted each other passionately, and kept up a fiery conversation. At dinner, go for the house specialty, and you'll never be disappointed. If you are in a restaurant and there isn't a house specialty listed on the menu, ask your server what the most popular items are on the menu. If you are as indecisive as I am, that's a good tactic to use when eating out. If struggling between two choices, talk your partner into ordering one of them and sharing. That's true love! I have included my favorite Italian dish that is a spin off from the entree I had the pleasure of eating that night. 'Amo Scallopini'!

In Italy, the meal isn't over until something sweet, or dolce, hits the tongue. After eating Italian food, I rarely have room for dessert, but I did plan a little dessert back in the hotel room. After dipping biscotti into a glass of Vin Santo, an Italian dessert wine, we kept the Italian passion going. Before we fell asleep, we made sure to call Guest Services and request coffee for the morning. No Italian morning is complete without a strong caffé or cappuccino! Buona Notte!

Chicken Scallopini with a Passion

This is a classic Italian dish taken to a new level with the addition of prosciutto, green onions and a mixture of Italian cheeses. It can be made in 30 minutes and is impressive enough for company.

Serves 4

Ingredients:
- 4 servings chicken breasts pounded thin
- 4 T unsalted butter
- 4 T olive oil
- 8 oz fresh mushrooms sliced
- 1 clove garlic minced
- 4 thin slices prosciutto
- ½ cup green onions chopped (green tops for garnish, white bottoms for sauce)
- ½ cup sweet Marsala wine
- ½ cup chicken broth
- 1 cup heavy cream
- salt and pepper to taste
- 1 cup shredded Italian cheeses
- angel hair pasta cooked according to directions

Directions:

1. Place the chicken between two pieces of plastic wrap and pound with a mallet. Pound to uniform in thickness ¼". Sprinkle with salt and pepper.
2. In a large ovenproof pan or cast iron skillet, heat 2 T butter and 2 T olive oil over medium heat. Add the mushrooms and sauté until tender, about 5 minutes. Remove with slotted spoon and set aside.

3. Heat the remaining 2 T butter and 2 T olive oil in the pan and add the chicken. Cook until browned turning once (about 7 minutes cooking time). Remove and set aside, keeping warm.
4. Add half the green onions (white part) and sauté 2 minutes scraping the bottom of the pan with a wooden spoon to loosen the browned bits. Add the garlic and continue cooking for 1 minute.
5. Add the Marsala and broth, bring to a boil, reduce the heat to a simmer, and cook until liquid is reduced by half. Whisk in the cream and season to taste with salt and pepper.
6. Add the mushrooms and chicken back in the pan and coat with the sauce. Arrange the chicken into four servings with mushrooms on top of the chicken. Place the prosciutto on top of each chicken piece. Next, add the cheese mixture on top of each chicken breast and place the skillet under the broiler just until the cheese melts. (If you don't have an ovenproof skillet, you can remove the chicken and place on a baking sheet to broil.) Finish the dish with the remaining green onions.
7. Serve this dish alongside angel hair pasta mixed with olive oil, salt and pepper and any remaining sauce.

Making Great Memories

Italian Style Toolbox

Hotel reservation (if doing an overnight getaway)
Italian restaurant reservation (feel free to use a fake Italian name)
"The Hot Italian Look and Attitude"
Portable music and speakers
LED candles
Italian light snacks, dessert and drink

Notes & Memories

11

Play Together, Stay Together

Introduction:

One of the things I find most attractive about my partner is his drive and desire for competition. Being an athlete all my life, I have also always had a thirst for healthy competition. Even in board games and in fun contests at parties, I will always fight to the bitter end.

Many couples may be surprised to discover that working-out and playing board games together could improve their love life. It's healthy to compete with your mate. Competition raises your heart rate and sends adrenaline through your veins, whether you're sweating or trying to work out complex mental challenges. Healthy competition is also a good way to test a person's character. What kind of loser are they and how do they treat others in competition? Let's fuel-up the competition and heat-up your relationship. Couples that play together, stay together!

This theme came from a comment I made to my partner about how everything is always a competition with him. I was probably frustrated at the time, but I realized how much fun we could have if we shifted the perspective to looking at competition as deliberate, intimate, and exciting! I thought it would be fun to fill our day with a variety of games and prizes, and it worked perfectly as an all-day birthday event. If you have small children, put them in a little referee uniform with a whistle or a pair of cheerleading pom-poms. It's healthy to let your kids see you having fun, using your imaginations, and competing with grins on your faces. Any way that you decide to do this, you'll have lots of fun, laughs and make great memories.

Warm-up

We need to get ready for game day, so try these creative ideas. As always, introduce the theme to your partner earlier in the week, so that you can both enjoy the anticipation leading up to the big day. One idea is to create a set of trading cards to share together (www.mytradingcards.com makes custom cards and sets). You can design a set for your partner and yourself, choosing from many different sports and leisure activities. If you can find old pictures from your spouse's high school sports teams or clubs, or an image of the mascot, that would be even better. Give out a different card to your partner throughout the week leading up to the competition.

In an attempt to antagonize my opponent, I teased my partner all week long by lifting weights in front of him, announcing when I went on my run, and mixing up post-workout protein drinks. Because we also love games and puzzles, I even created a wordsearch with words for my game plan, which was very easy to do with a puzzle maker online.

Game Day Uniform:

Dressing like an athlete is crucial for this day. Here are some ideas to make your uniform fit with today's theme:

- Purchase a shirt from your mate's high school and have his name printed on it. Most high schools have online stores, or you could look into a local screen printing store in his hometown. If your honey has been out of high school a long time, he or she will probably love the extra effort you put into this. Be sure to have your high school shirt or college shirt as well.
- Purchase a team shirt from your favorite professional team.
- Design your sports shirts or dress as superheroes
- Find retro uniforms complete with knee-high socks, headbands or wristbands. Maybe you still have an old high school uniform.
- Complete your game-face with under-the-eye reflective face paint, hair in a ponytail, sports cap, sneakers, and sweatbands. Look as sporty as possible.

Post-game Uniform

Your birthday boy may want to forfeit his entire game day and go directly to the final match when he learns about your post-game attire. Go to my website, www.makinggreatmemories.com/shop/ where I direct you to lots of choices for the sexiest sportswear and lingerie. If anything, a sexy sports bra could throw off your competition and put you in the winner's bracket!

The Playing Field

This day would be incomplete without a proper, adrenaline-pumping soundtrack. I'm thinking deep bass lines and eighties jams, like "The Final Countdown" by Europe. Lots of the best jock jams or energy-boosting rock came out during the eighties and nineties, so you could even just select or create a playlist from that era. Find the genre that gets you moving and shaking and hook your device up to some blasting speakers.

Before the competition begins, get your half-time snacks ready. I suggest plenty of Gatorade, protein bars and cut-up oranges.

The Game Plan

There are so many ways you can play with this idea, and I'm going to offer a ton of suggestions. Ultimately you can decide how you want your competition to go and how you want to alter the theme. Everyone is different, so customize the experience to what feels right for you today. The good news is that you could do this day all over again and have another unique experience. If you are planning to do this as a birthday celebration, then you may want to purchase games as presents and open them as you go through the competition.

Being the competitor that I am, I created a scoreboard using a chalkboard. Keeping score isn't necessarily for everyone, but I had fun doing it. I also had a prize for every competition we did. They were silly, simple prizes, and some that were related to the theme or game. In corn hole, for instance, the winner wins a bag of popcorn or Cracker Jack. The winner in Chinese checkers wins a fortune cookie. You could also purchase (from a party store) award medals, ribbons and packs of plastic award trophies.

I've broken the competition into indoor and outdoor activities and also away-games. There are games of skill and strategy and, of course, there are a few silly games too. I've also included a mix of games requiring a little financial investment and games you can do for free. It's all up to you!

Indoor Competition:

Scrabble
Yahtzee
Checkers, Chinese Checkers
Backgammon
Chess
Rummikub
Jenga
Card games like Fish, War, Speed, Cribbage and Rummy
Memory

Games requiring more activity - great in the winter or on a rainy day:
Hopscotch- Play in the garage or basement. Create with chalk and use a coin or bean bag.
Indoor basketball- Use rolled up socks and a bucket or a *Nerf* hoop and ball for the back of a door
Play *Wii* - lots of physical games available on *Wii*
Ping-pong
Billiard pool
Pinball machine

Outdoor Competition:

Basketball - Play "Around the World" or PIG
Corn Hole (I had one custom made for the birthday present with a big red ribbon)
Ladderball
Horseshoes
Bocce Ball

Washer Toss
Badminton
Croquet
Pickleball

Away Games:
Miniature Golf
Go Karts
Bowling
Video Arcade for skeeball and air hockey, etc

Food:

No theme is complete without planning for fun food and drink. I think the perfect way to start the day is with the breakfast of champions -WHEATIES! Now if you want to make a great memory today, plan this ahead of time - visit the Wheaties website and find the contact page where you can upload a picture of the birthday star onto a box of Wheaties. For a small fee, you can have your very own Wheaties.

Recipes

I also suggest starting the day with delicious, high-energy smoothies:

Good Morning Smoothie

Serves: 1

Ingredients:
- ½ cup chopped ice
- ½ cup frozen blueberries (could use strawberries, bananas, peaches, oranges, etc.)
- ½. cup vanilla yogurt
- ½ cup coconut milk
- 1T honey
- 1-2 T protein powder

Directions: Blend until smooth.

Tropical Deliciousness

Serves: 1

Ingredients:
- 1 cup super greens (spinach and kale)
- half a banana
- ½ cup chunk pineapple
- ½ cup frozen strawberries
- ½ cup coconut milk or vanilla yogurt
- ½ cup chopped ice
- 1-2 T protein powder

Directions: Blend until smooth.

Post-Workout Drink

Any high endurance athlete will tell you about the importance of recovery and refueling following an intense workout. The number one choice among many athletes, myself included, is fat-free chocolate milk. High in carbohydrates and protein, it's the perfect choice for replenishing tired muscles. Depending on the intensity of your day, here's an idea for an adult version of chocolate milk, which is a nice suggestion for the next round of competition, the food!

Adult Chocolate Milk

Serving 2

Ingredients:
- 2 oz Irish Cream
- 2 oz Coffee Liqueur
- 2 oz Chocolate Liqueur
- 1 oz Vodka
- 2 oz milk
- Ice

Directions:
Place all ingredients except ice into a container and stir well. Put ice in a glass tumbler or favorite sports team glass and pour cocktail over the ice. Garnish with a sports team swizzle stick.

The Dinner Menu of Champions

The competition continues with dinner. In the format of the popular Food Network show, "Chopped," you and your partner will enjoy challenging each other in the kitchen. Without making this too complicated, together find 12 random ingredients from your pantry or refrigerator and place them out on the counter or in a basket as done on the show. Decide who will make the appetizer and who will make the main course. If you want this to be a bigger event, then you can challenge each other with three rounds and maybe have your kids be the judges. I love the mini version, because I prefer small cleanups over huge messes! My partner did the appetizer, and I made the main course. It's not necessarily a challenge, but it's fun all the same. We took turns selecting from our pile of random ingredients, which includes four in each course. The "FINAL 4" elements went to the final dessert round which we had fun creating together. While we were doing this, I had "Chopped" playing in the background since my partner had never even seen the show. The music and clock ticking added to the atmosphere, so put on your aprons, set a timer for 30 minutes and let the competition begin!

Friendly Scrimmage and Sports Award Presentation

Being a great athlete means you must have endurance, so hopefully you still have energy left for a little friendly competition in the bedroom. If not, make sure you schedule a scrimmage soon! Meet your competition in the bedroom with your sexy sports lingerie and the final adult board game *The Bedroom Game* (link at my website). A bedroom is also a perfect place for the awards presentation. The party store had a plastic trophy which I gave to my partner for being my most valuable player. Being exhausted from a full day of competition, we found cuddling on the sofa and watching a movie was the perfect ending to our game day.

Consider these competition movies classics:

Dodgeball
Semi-Pro
Bring It On
Cool Runnings
Chariots of Fire
Foxcatcher

Best in Show
Hoosiers
Pitch Perfect
Billy Fisher
McFarland
Rocky

Making Great Memories

Play Together, Stay Together Toolbox

Many of the following items can be found at:
www.makinggreatmemories.com/shop/

Trading Cards
Puzzle Maker
Uniforms
Game day music
Scoreboard
Silly prizes
Boardgames
Lawn Games
Chopped items and basket
Sports lingerie or costume
Adult bedroom boardgame

Notes & Memories

12

British Birthday Invasion

Introduction

Most of my life, I have found it more fulfilling to create a special birthday memory than to give gifts. Although gifts are often a part of that memory, they needn't be an extravagant expenditure. Most people will remember the experience over the gifts.

My significant other is of British heritage, so I thought it would be fun to research his ancestry and see what I could do to create a unique birthday celebration. As with many themes, once I got rolling with this one, I couldn't stop. So, if this seems a little much, just remember to take what you want and leave the rest . . . maybe for another celebration. I don't know if it is because I live in New England, but once I got started, I was amazed by how many British pieces came together for this theme. That's what will get your blood flowing, and what makes these theme nights just as much fun to give as to receive—that rush of joy when everything comes together magically.

The Quest for the Crest

I began my quest for the ultimate British Invasion by researching websites that allow you to create family crests on just about anything. You can create your own coat of arms if you like, which could be great fun for the whole family, kids included. I found it fascinating to connect these historical names with their meanings and discover the traditional family crests. As a gift, I chose a poster of the genealogy of my partner's name and also a beautiful porcelain stein featuring his family crest which I found at www.allfamilycrests.com. I also began researching websites that sold anything British. To my surprise, I found a local store right in my state that featured all-British items. If that happened for me, chances are there's a store like this near you too! If not, you can also order from their website, www.britishgoods.com.

The British are coming, The British are coming!

We decided to split the festivities into two consecutive evenings, so the day before my husband's birthday, I took him to a newly-opened restaurant in town. Before we went to the eatery, we got the birthday started with a traditional British cocktail featuring Pimm's and Beefeater. A little appetizer of cucumber sandwiches served with Queen napkins also helped establish the birthday theme.

Good Morning Luv!

Start the day by treating your royal birthday king or queen to crumpets, morello cherry jam, and English Breakfast Tea (all items I found at Trader Joe's). Place them on a serving tray alongside a handwritten note wishing your mate a brilliant birthday. You can also share a few details about the royal birthday celebration you have planned for the evening.

British Fun

If you enjoy golf, I suggest finding a "Links" course in your area. Bring along cucumber sandwiches and Bass Ale or Carling. Watch the British Open. Refer to my theme on golf for further ideas and information. Go to a Shakespearean play or read Shakespeare's love sonnets to each other. Speak in a British accent all day. Dress all in white and play croquet. Croquet is a fabulous game that took England by storm in the 1860's and then spread overseas. If the timing is right, many communities have annual Highland Games and Medieval festivals. Grab your fancy garden hat and find a country inn that features a traditional English tea service in their garden. Polo, anyone?

British Invasion:

Set the music genre to British Invasion. Favorite Brits include The Beatles, Rolling Stones, Pink Floyd, The Who, Elton John, Eric Clapton, Rod Stewart, Adele, Amy Winehouse, David Bowie, Sam Smith.

Who Needs Swag When You've Got MOJO?

For this theme, you can get creative and goofy with your outfit. I went for trendy and wore a red t-shirt that had, "Keep Calm and Carry On" written across my chest and completed my look with a rhinestone tiara. I found the shirt at the British Goods store. I also found a new bath towel there, which I wrapped around my hubby that looks like a kilt. It was a fabulous gift that he still likes to wear while strutting around our castle. You could also consider purchasing a sexy British costume or undergarment. Go to my website www.makinggreatmemories.com/shop/ where I provide a link to these hot British items. Oh, behave!

Another Gift Idea

If your partner is a lover of scotch, consider watching the *60 Minutes* episode featuring Bob Simon's final interview at Whiskey Island in Scotland. It's a wonderful story that inspired me to purchase a very special scotch from that region, which I paired with a distinct Scotch glass and gifted to my British babe.

High Tea

High Tea happens around six in the evening and is a traditional and substantial meal that the British enjoy with family or friends. I created a unique setting around the coffee table featuring a ploughman's lunch with several items I found at the British Goods store. My special birthday bloke had a traditional British beer in his new family crest stein, and I drank a Vesper Martini, an iconic favorite of James Bond. The ploughman's lunch could include a crusty bread or stotty cake with an English cheddar cheese, ploughman's relish, pickled onions, salty radish, and celery, along with an assortment of candies and digestives. If you have room in your bellies, consider a birthday dinner featuring any of the following traditional English meals; shepherd's pie, Welsh rarebit, bangers and mash, or fish and chips with mushy peas. I went the easy route with a frozen meat pie from The British

Goods store, but I've included one of my husband's favorite comfort foods in the recipe section of this theme. Also, consider researching recipes from the following British chefs: Jamie Oliver, Gordon Ramsay, Nigella Lawson and Mary Berry.

Pimm's Cup

This cocktail was invented by James Pimm and is a traditional English drink at cricket matches.

Servings: A pitcher

Ingredients:
- 1 orange, cut into half moons
- 1 lemon, cut into half moons
- English cucumber washed and cut into several slices and 3 inch spears for garnish
- 1 cup Pimm's
- 2 cups lemon-lime soda
- sprigs of mint
- gin (optional)

Directions:
Fill a pitcher ¼ full of ice, then layer with lemon, orange and cucumber. Repeat layer. Pour Pimm's and soda over layers. Add mint leaves. To serve: Pour cocktail in tall glass and add fruit slices along with a cucumber spear. Additional kick: add a shot of gin (preferably an English gin like Beefeater).

Vesper Martini

This drink was invented by Ian Fleming in the 1953 James Bond novel, Casino Royale.

Three measures of Gordon's (gin), one of vodka, half a measure of Kina Lillet. Shake it very well until it's ice-cold, then add a large thin slice of lemon peel served in a deep champagne goblet.

English Tea Cucumber Sandwiches

Ingredients:
- 1 English cucumber, peeled and thinly sliced
- 4 oz cream cheese, softened
- 2T mayonnaise
- dash onion salt
- dash Worcestershire sauce
- ½ tsp minced garlic
- 1 tsp fresh minced dill
- white bread cut into rounds with a cookie cutter

Directions:

1. Place the cucumber slices between 2 paper towels and set in a colander so the liquid can drain, about 10 minutes.
2. Mix the remaining ingredients together in a bowl until smooth. Spread the cream cheese mixture on the bread rounds, then a cucumber slice, and finish with another bread round. Sprinkle lightly with paprika.

Shepherd's Pie (Cottage Pie) with Caramelized Onion

This is one of our favorite comfort foods. Served in a pie plate, this recipe could easily be doubled to please a crowd and prepared in a 9x13 baking pan. Leftovers are great to freeze for a quick weeknight meal.

Servings: 4-6

Ingredients:
- 2 T butter (divided)
- 2 T olive oil (divided)
- 1 large onion ½ chopped, ½ sliced (for caramelized onion)
- 2 carrots sliced
- 1 clove garlic minced
- 1 T tomato catsup
- 1 lb ground beef or lamb
- 1 1/2 T cornstarch or flour
- 1 T worcestershire sauce
- 1/2 cup beef stock
- 1 cup frozen peas thawed
- 1/2 cup frozen white corn thawed
- salt and fresh ground pepper

Cheesy mashed potatoes:
- 2 pounds Yukon gold potatoes, peeled and quartered
- 2 T butter
- 1/3 cup half and half, heavy cream or milk
- 1/2 cup grated sharp cheddar cheese
- salt and pepper

Directions:

1. Begin recipe by placing potatoes in a saucepan with salted cold water and bring to boil. Cook until soft, about 20-30 minutes. Drain and keep in pan for mashing. Start next part of recipe while potatoes are cooking.
2. Preheat oven 400 degrees.
3. To caramelize the onions for the topping; melt 1 T butter and 1 T oil in large skillet over medium-high heat. Add only the sliced onions from half the onion. Sauté until brown, turn down the heat to low, then add ½ tsp kosher salt and cook until golden about 15 minutes. Remove from pan and start next step.
4. In the same skillet, add the remaining 1 T butter and 1 T olive oil sautéing the remaining chopped onion and carrots about 10 minutes. Add the garlic and salt and pepper.
5. Once vegetables have softened, add the tomato catsup and ground beef, cooking until no longer pink.
6. Add the cornstarch to the meat followed by the worcestershire sauce and the beef stock. Simmer 10 minutes.
7. Add the peas and corn, heat thoroughly, then transfer to a 9" deep pie plate.
8. Once the potatoes are done and drained, add to the saucepan along with the potatoes, butter, cream, salt and pepper and mash or beat until smooth. Add more cream if necessary. Finally, stir in the cheddar cheese and mix well.
9. Spread cheesy mashed potatoes over the meat mixture, cover with the caramelized onions and bake until browned about 20 minutes.

MAKING GREAT MEMORIES

Dessert:

Traditional desserts are Eton Mess and Black Forest Gateau. If time is in short supply, consider purchasing a chocolate gateau cake and filling the top with morello cherries (both available at Trader Joe's). My favorite purchase at the British Goods Store was a solar-powered Queen Elizabeth figurine with a waving hand, which I used as a cake topper. In my best British accent, I sang happy birthday to my prince charming.

Cuddle time:

Great British movie favorites include:

> *James Bond*
> *Austin Powers series*
> *The King's Speech*
> *Monty Python* films
> *Full Monty*
> *Billy Elliot*
> *Harry Potter*
> *Pride and Prejudice*
> British "telly" suggestions:
> *Downton Abbey*
> *Benny Hill*
> *Doctor Who*
> *Game of Thrones.*

Making Great Memories

British Birthday Invasion Toolbox

Many of the following items can be found at:
www.makinggreatmemories.com/shop/

Allfamilycrests.com Coat of arms/family crests
British Goods (my personal list)
"Keep Calm and Carry On" t-shirt
Kilt towel
British costume or undergarments
"A Wee Dram" scotch glass
English tea and jam
Ploughman's pickles and relish
Candies and digestives
English cheddar cheese
Meat pie
Pimm's, Beefeater, Bass Ale, Scotch from Whiskey Island
The Queen solar figurine
British birthday cake

Cheerio!!

Notes & Memories

Recipe Index

CHAPTER 1 TROPICAL ISLAND STAYCATION

- Piña Colada 19
- Coconut Shrimp 20
- Caribbean Jerk Seasoning 21
- Easy Tropical Salsa 21
- Orange Dipping Sauce 21
- Island Teriyaki Chicken for Two 22
- Caribbean Rice with Roasted/ Grilled Vegetables 23
- Warm Banana in Rum Sauce with Coconut Ice cream and Macadamia Sprinkle 24

CHAPTER 2 VALENTINE'S DAY WITH A FRENCH TWIST

- The French 75 Cocktail 33
- French Onion Soup 34
- Crudité with French Vinaigrette 36
- Filet of Beef Au Poivre 37
- Chicken Cordon Bleu 38
- Fingerling Potatoes 39
- Haricots Verts 39
- Profiteroles 41

CHAPTER 3 SPRING INTO LOVE WITH GOLF

- Arnold Palmer 51
- Pimento Cheese Spread 52
- Fried Green Tomatoes 53
- Southern Buttermilk Biscuits 54
- Black Eyed Pea Salad 55
- Georgia Peach Ice Cream Sandwiches 56

CHAPTER 4 FRUGAL FUN FRIDAY

- Spanish Sangria ... 65
- Hummus ... 66
- Romaine Salad with Feta and Orange ... 67
- Lemon/Shallot Vinaigrette ... 67
- Balsamic/Dijon Vinaigrette ... 67
- Creamy Parmesan Dressing ... 67
- One-Pot Bacon Top Roast Chicken ... 68
- Chocolate Pudding ... 70
- Chicken Stock ... 71
- Mom's Homemade Chicken Soup ... 72
- Allie's Chicken Salad ... 73
- Homemade Raspberry Cordial ... 74
- Homemade Coffee Liqueur ... 75
- Homemade Irish Cream Liqueur ... 76

CHAPTER 5 WHEN A MAN LOVES A WOMAN (MAN PLAN)

- Pan-Seared Salmon ... 89
- Oven-Roasted Vegetables ... 89
- New York Strip Steak with Herb Butter ... 91
- Oven Baked Potatoes ... 91
- So-Easy Chocolate Cream Pie ... 93

CHAPTER 6 FROM PALETTE TO PALATE

- The Bellini Cocktail ... 104
- Carpaccio ... 104
- Cubist Salad ... 105
- Beach Rose Potatoes ... 106
- Pan-Seared Scallops ... 108
- LOVE Brownie Silhouette ... 109

CHAPTER 7 ANNIVERSARY QUICKIE

Lemon Drop Martini 119
Red Velvet Heart Cake.. 121
Cream Cheese Frosting 122

CHAPTER 8 JAPANEASY

Green Tea Martini 131
Vegetable Sushi Rolls 132
Sushi Dipping Sauce 134

CHAPTER 9 ROLEPLAY GETAWAY: COWBOY UP!

Prickly Pear Cactus Margarita 144
Easy Cowboy Beans 146
Chipotle Slaw.. 147
Cheesy Jalapeno Cornbread 148
Texas Sheet Cake 149

CHAPTER 10 ROLE PLAY GETAWAY: ITALIAN STYLE

Chicken Scallopini with a Passion 158

CHAPTER 11 BIRTHDAY COMPETITION

Good Morning Smoothie... 168
Tropical Deliciousness 168
Adult Chocolate Milk 169

CHAPTER 12 BRITISH BIRTHDAY INVASION

Pimm's Cup Cocktail 178
Vesper Martini 179
English Tea Cucumber Sandwiches... 179
Shepherd's Pie (Cottage Pie) 180

Final Thoughts

I am so honored you took the time to read this book and I sincerely hope you've been inspired to create your own magic and memories. If you have an idea for a theme or an experience you would like to share, I would LOVE to hear from you! Please feel free to contact me @

Website www.Makinggreatmemories.com
Blog /www.makinggreatmemories.com/blog/
Facebook www.facebook.com/queenoftheme/
YouTube http://www.makinggreatmemories.com/videos
Pinterest https://www.pinterest.com/LCGreatorex/
Subscribe to Making Great Memories Newsletter

Coming soon!
    Making Great Memories: The Date Night Collection VOL 2

About The Author

An educator of 27 years and a perpetual planner, LC Greatorex is calling for couples, friends and families across America to bring intimacy and entertainment back into quality time! Affectionately known as the "Queen of Theme," LC used her teaching expertise and years of hosting to compile the *Making Great Memorie*s book series and vlog, full to the brim with professional tips on executing captivating nights and unforgettable experiences. LC offers readers the complete package of brainstorming, budgeting and creating the perfect memory, whether it be a girlfriend theme party or a tropical romantic dinner. When LC isn't scheming her next theme or spending time with family, you will find her somewhere in the US on a golf course, eating with the locals or digging deep into thrift stores and clam flats.

Acknowledgments and Gratitude

First of all, I need to recognize that this book would not have been possible if it wasn't for the big G and the little g...God and google.

Thank you to my dear friends, Laura Kinney, Lisa Adkison and Lynn Gierie. Laura who walked and talked with me for miles and miles, listening to all my ideas and supporting me so enthusiastically with her endless giggles and interest. Lisa, who always made time to pray with me, especially in the darkest of times, and helped me understand the incredible power of faith. Lynn, who took the time to proofread my manuscript and more importantly, changed the direction of my life when she insisted I give love a second chance.

A big shout-out to the talented team of young women who made Making Great Memories possible. Zoe Romano, who not only took my words and shaped them into a book, she continually reinforced my concept with her youthful enthusiasm. Amanda McKrell for her candid insight and professional consulting and editing services. Melissa Bennett, for her patience and brilliance with website design and social media expertise, and Tatiana Fernandez, for the book cover design.

It is with immense gratitude that I would like to acknowledge Jason Anderson from Polgarus Studio for his high-quality work, patience, professionalism, and expertise in book formatting.

Very special thanks to my family, espccially Mom and Dad, who have inspired me with their deep love and commitment to marriage over 50 years. Also, to my daughter Alyssa, whose honesty and opinion I was forever seeking. I am grateful and blessed for all the wonderful relationships I've had throughout my life and which helped lay the foundation for Making Great Memories.

Finally, I am most grateful for my husband, Jim, the love of my life. Thank you for igniting this incredible passion, fueled by our many Friday date nights, and also for the blending of our beautiful families —inspiration for Making Great Memories to come.

Printed in Poland
by Amazon Fulfillment
Poland Sp. z o.o., Wrocław